Contents of a Curious Mind

Contents of a Curious Mind

By
Scott
Robertson

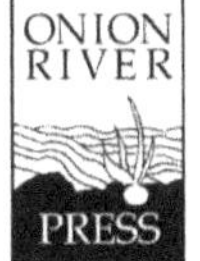

Onion River Press
89 Church Street
Burlington, VT 05401

info@onionriverpress.com
www.onionriverpress.com
ISBN: 978-1-966607-40-3

Library of Congress Control Number: 2026903213

I would like to dedicate this book to thrice U.S. Poet Laureate Robert Pinsky, Humorist Steven Wright, and the gang of artists, writers, and editors that ever graced the pages of *MAD* Magazine.

Table of Contents

Foreword

Contents of a Curious Mind is an evocative confluence of poems, thoughts and observations: sketches (brief commentaries on human behavior); a segment on the clues and realities that make you aware that you are getting older; and a collection of cartoons that reflect the mannerisms, foibles, and vagaries of, once again, our fellow man. Formed sporadically over a 54-year period in the cranium of the now-seventy-three-year-old upstart and retired commercial banker, yours truly Scott Robertson.

So, just how and why did I manage to produce such a curious compilation of verse, witticisms, narratives, and cartoon depictions? you may ask.

The famous Bard of Avon once famously observed, "All the world is a stage, and all the men and women merely players." And, as we all know, he quite convincingly and effectively parlayed that perception into a rather memorable and sustainable series of plays and poems that reflected and encompassed the joys and struggles, beliefs and uncertainties, and promises and pitfalls of the universal experiences that make up the human condition.

Heck. For as long as I can remember, I've been in that audience: front and center, staring up at that stage, taking in every rehearsal, every matinee, and every opening night possible. For I am the anonymous witness, silently watching and studying the naturally spontaneous, wonderfully extemporaneous, and impromptu musings; movements and machinations of mankind playing out before me; the unobtrusive observer and self-imposed scribe and reporter of this panoply of odd and quirky habits and absurd inclinations; the cavalcade of quotable monologues and dialogues; and the endless tendencies, propensities, and idiosyncrasies of my fellow man. Making sure to diligently file it all away in a cerebral vault and reinforcingly jot them down on the back of the program for preservation.

I've always had a lot on my mind, with no particular place to put it all. Plus, I have always wanted to know exactly what people think of what my take is on the everyday behavioral residue that people knowingly or unwittingly cast and scatter and seed across the cultural and societal landscape.

And that is why I write. I write to invite you, all of you, to sit with me in that audience, to share what I observe of those players; perceive my take on humanity and, if you dare, endeavor to comprehend just how the heck my mind works!

My hope is that it's as much fun for you to read as it was for me to write.

Poetry

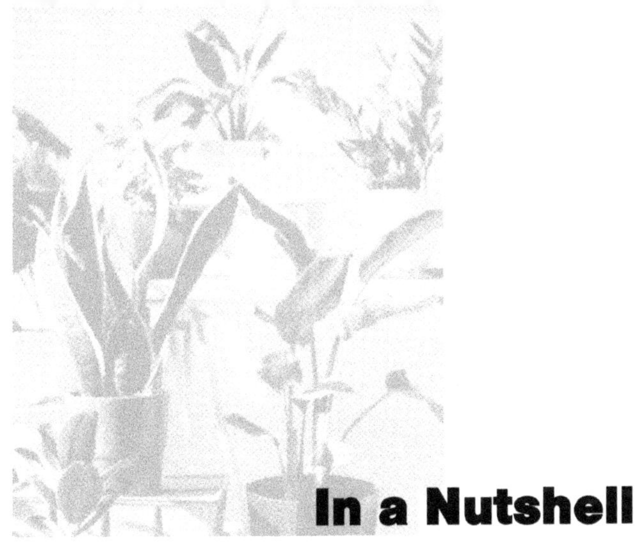

In a Nutshell

I drink in moderation,

Don't smoke too many joints;

It's safe to say I don't raise much fuss

Or argue many points.

Respectful of my elders,

Tolerant of my kin;

And as such I don't do much

When required to fit in.

I prefer cleanliness to godliness

And potted-plants to politics;

For the news I peruse the headlines

And that generally will suffice,

It's when I ingest the rest of the text

That makes me lie awake at night.

To Wit:

As a baseball little leaguer

I made the all-star teams;

In basketball I could not dunk

But made a lot of threes;

In football, the coach got in my face

'Cuz I wouldn't play with pain,

And at the age of ten years old I retired from the game.

As a kid in high school

Lost interest and skipped many classes

Getting mostly Cs and Ds,

Then I got a pair of glasses

And watched my grade point average climb to

mostly As and Bs.

From there to a stint in art school

Where the goal is to draw a nude model,

in all her proper perspective,

And since my skills were more abstract, with the

lines all generally skewed,

In lieu what I drew was a female cartoon clad in

just her birthday suit.

And when leaning over my shoulder to see how he

should respond,

The prominent art professor curiously intoned:

"So that's how Betty Rubble looks with absolutely no clothes on."

Graduating college, armed with knowledge and aplomb,

The sheepskin proved not helpful for I could not land a job,

And since Viet Nam was over, I enlisted with Uncle Sam.

I did not want a rifle or an extended tour at sea,

The Air Force was the option, or then again it seemed;

The recruiter said I'd enter a full-fledged officer,

And test scores attached the post of aerial photographer;

But the excitement, hope, and promise ultimately were nixed,

Not for something that I did,

It was just because their problem was

I had asthma as a kid.

Desperate for a paycheck

Or alas perhaps a career,

I needed a hook or a strategy that would grab somebody's ear.

So, I honed and shaped my resume with key words

    that might sell;

Persuasive at the interview I finally got the call

And landed squarely behind a desk at a prominent S & L.

And, now, after forty-two years in banking,

Mostly restructuring delinquent loans,

I traded in the rat race for the tranquility of home.

The Naysayers sigh and roll their eyes,

Alluding to they would lose their minds if ever

forced to fill the time.

Contented with book and pen and the promise of every day,

It's safe to say I've never had to ever think that way.

And admittedly out of line with most of mankind

I live by what I find to be the perfect anecdote:

That being it's best to push the box and think

outside the envelope.

A Reflection of Light

All that we appear is but a reflection of light;
All that we are is but a measure of substance;
And all that we shall become
Is but an interpretation of time.

The Energy of Her Essence

And when he writes for her,

The words Explode upon the page,

And structure and content

Are effortless;

And although

He has never touched her hand nor cheek,

He cradles her image from a distance

And is consumed by

The energy of her essence.

You Are Away

I am propped on the couch watching the screen,

Aware that you are away;

I fiddle and click; shift and click; maneuver and click.

And then again. And then again.

Senses dulled I study a wall, the ceiling, the floor.

And then again. And then again.

I relocate to the kitchen. Mumbled parlance.

Anxious and unfulfilled in your absence

I select a window to stare from.

And then another.

And then another.

I descend the stairs to lie on our bed;

Body fully stretched, inhaling and holding-breath.

Slowly exhaling I attempt to relax;

Failing, I fidget and toss and squirm and protract.

And then again. And then again.

To calm the restlessness,

Palms pressed gently against closed eyes,

I invite sleep to void your absence.

I am in your presence

as I drift to thoughts of moments shared:

On the ferry from Hyannis to Nantucket

And its mirrored return;

Or across the street from our coastal ocean home,

Selecting, collecting beachstone with casual discern;

The least tern's flair in defense of its nest,

Or a catbird's feathered illusion

Our silent request.

I see you in the garden

Planting tomatoes and sewing seed,

And—sorry Sweetie—the expectation of pulling weed,

Over and over, and over again.

And on warm, calm summer afternoons at one o'clock

    or two o'clock,

Without timepiece or word, we know it's time

To make our scheduled assent to our cedar deck

To lunch on old favorites of iced tea and chips and BLTs.

Sitting on deck chairs, side by side,

I watch you read the paper or a magazine,

Your New York Times or Bon Appetit,

And I watch the sea birds: sea gull and skimmer and cormorant,

Dip and dive and soar and shift

On the desirable, westerly sea breeze currents

Above the light-blue Atlantic

And its own conducive currents from the south.

And then, absent of timepiece or word or hint of indication,

A sudden auspicious eerie calm envelops the coastal air.

We listen, and then lock eyes, inherently knowing that it is
> *three o'clock:*

When the wind abruptly, suddenly surges and selfishly shifts stiff
> *from the southeast;*

Instantly chilling and churning, coercing and intimidating the
> *unwitting summer air;*

Scattering the gulls and shattering the waves,

Ultimately pursuing and pushing and propelling us into
> *the kitchen.*

Engaged, we select a window to watch Nature's drama unfold:

Seabirds, with feathers sealed against perfect aerodynamic forms,

Diligently fight the wind, again and again;

Failing, chattering angrily, they are chased from the ocean

To the river to the west.

Ocean water, now, suddenly—an indignant, dark foamy green,

Gallantly swells to fight and repel the petulant wind again
> *and again.*

Failing, the swells are coerced and reversed,

Summarily dismissed to the north and west.

We move to another window,

And then another. And then another.

A solitary lone rogue whitecap climbs and crests and summarily

hurtles itself against the seawall with a thunderous thud

Sending sea spray soaring and scattering into the whirling and
  whimsical wind.
Appeased and fatigued from nature's truculent display
We then descend the stairs to lie on our bed,
To embrace and hold tight each other.
Warm in sweatshirts and each other's arms
We kiss and know how lucky we are to have,
If nothing else, each other.
We kiss. We kiss.
And then again. And then again.
Awake. I am missing you.
Although you are not here beside me
I roll to your side, as is my ritual
When you are there,
To clutch and caress and consume your image.
And then again. And then again.

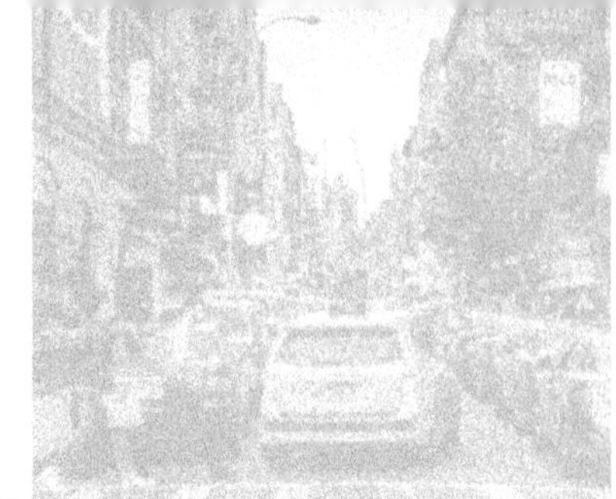

A Remarkable Remnant

While in New York, heading down 1st Avenue,

I paused to just glance

At all that enhanced this Winter afternoon:

The stiff-staggering, crisp-blue wind;

The small-piercing, eye-drop-yellow sun;

The curious, exotic swirling aroma

Of ethnic culinary blend;

The steadfast habitual-ritual

Of the wood-burning bum 'neath the 59th Street Bridge

And the outlandish contrast

Of silly, scurrying, furriered women.

And the cab that slows

To subtly scheme and contrive me to ride,

But my expression conveys that I must stay outside;

To prolong and stay in this instance,

In the essence of this omnipresence that, obliged,

Must now fade to black from its yellow and blue;

And in the midst an awareness ensues

That I must continue down the avenue,

To reflect on the beauty of this afternoon

As when reflecting the image of what once was you.

Summer Storm:

On and on through summer storm

Of glistening dark-green earth

And smokey greased-streaked steel-gray sky;

Leaning over the steering wheel,

Peering, squinting through the dull-thud splatter

On the rain-peppered glass,

Wipers at full speed whip back and forth

In rapid-rubbing staccato succession,

Leaving only the slowly dissipating shadowy rubber remnants

Of their presence.

The Perfect Perennial

Because of you
I shall never know
The predictable complacency that life can bestow:
As the unquestioned cadence of timepiece theme
Or resilient redundance of pendulum swing;
The syllabic structure of Haiku rhyme
Or encumbering ethic of sonnet line.
You're an exciting, effortless deep-breath,
A solicited pulse,
The pure-rush of heart beat,
The sweet feel of love;
You're a balanced cohesion
Of symmetrical blend,
The perfect union,
The perfect friend.
Our incredible life,
Conceived by fate and confirmed by vow
Is a unique reinforced time-cell of one-year now;
An annual reflection
Of a back porch refrain,
Now a life-time observance
Forever sustained.

I Am Whisked Away by Nothing More

I am whisked away by nothing more

Than the ebb-and-flow and subtle allure

Of the calm, comforting, mid-night breeze-current

Emanating from the dark like some virtual, benevolent serpent

As it subtly shifts and slithers past an illumed deck-sconce

Of relinquished, muted-yellow tint.

Finding its way to my passive, reclined repose,

It hints a promise of response

To absorb and assuage and abstain the pain:

It's cool breath subtly brushing the nape

Of my partially exposed neck;

A brief pause and then the wispy-whip

Of its mythical torso and tail

As it scales my shoulders and rubs my back.

Then flowing—up and over and around

the veiled, gauzy three-quarter moon—

Now achieving its apex—exposed in the night sky

By the hiding-antithetic sun,

Then dipping down to nudge and expose an ocean

Now flood-lit and festooned as a shimmering jewel.

In Search of Beachstone

On unscheduled Summer mornings long before noon,

Climbing stairway of liquid-stained cedar grain;

Climbing up-and-over composite stone and cemented wall,

Landing just inside the spreading dune

We watch the gulls soar and fall.

Standing bare-foot in the sun-warmed and pliant sand

We scan the glitter and shine of the expanding and contracting

Silica and quartz foreground,

The final, granular coastal segment of land,

And pass-through dune's worn pathway absent of sound.

Embanked passage flanked by impromptu bunches of flowering

Seagrass and reed, like metronomes swaying left and right

In cadence and rhythm with the shifting breeze.

Captured by the moment, we search for each other and hold

hands tight;

We are in search of beachstone:

Born from igneous and metamorphic;

Of conglomerate and sedimentary,

Cut and polished as if from Earth's own lapidary.

Traversing down and across the undulant beach,

In sight of sea's blue and acrobatic compliant fabric,

Shiny and wet compacted mineral morsels appear within reach

To be plucked and pocketed for color and grain divergent

Or for shape abstract or geometric.

Now shoulder-sloped from capacity weight of brim-filled

Shoulder-strapped fabric sack,

We trudge up-beach through dune pass with toes splayed

To light on up-step over wall

With only mind's-eye looking back.

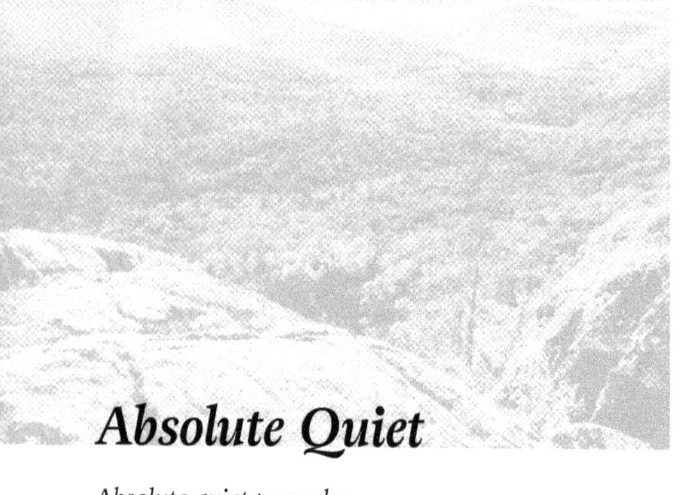

Absolute Quiet

Absolute quiet pervades

As the hushed Eastern-white pine and paper-bark birch

    fail to sway

In this wind-less and cloud-laden late summer afternoon;

Clouds plume, contract and expand

To form metaphoric shapes sublime

That only imagination can define.

Nature dominates the moment

As I dangle my toes in the sun-warmed pool

That lies within the meadow around the back

At the inn above Woodstock;

Leaning-lying back on the cement deck,

Eyes close and I am absent of rule.

Tree-scaped, verdant forest Catskill Mountain periphery

Envelopes and consumes the echo of my footsteps,

and now-contented energy,

As I traverse its paths in presence solitary,

Aligned, a mutual respect unfolds within the inner-circumference

Of the omnipresent and calming scenery.

And now, at base of graded dirt path's turn—a slight angle

> *to the right,*

The serene, burnt-copper blue and forest-green visage

Of Cooper Lake enters my line of sight.

And in the foreground, tree-stands and brush

Speckled with leaf and needle and flower

Line and defend the Lake's irregular shoreline and

> *undulating contour.*

And overhead, against the now graying-blue sky,

Tawny-tinted, white billowed puffs subtly ply

From behind the span of wavy, rounded woodland peaks

Adding to the peace and solace that I have come to seek.

And now, as I stretch to rest on warm polished stone,

That line the mirrored bank,

I inhale deep to memory the panorama

And elicit a silent thanks

For the irreplaceable, confluent gift

That has been provided me

Of which camera's eye could never see.

A Friend:

Shares, without taking;

Questions, without doubting;

Speaks, without demanding;

Listens, without judging;

Touches, without intruding;

Loves, without possessing.

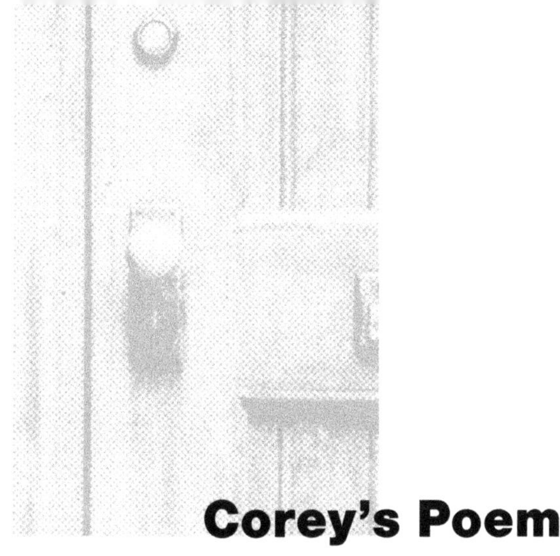

Corey's Poem

A Birthday is a good time To reflect on:

What has happened and what will be;

What you saw and what you'll see;

What you were and what you'll be;

Unlocked doors and new found keys.

A Most Memorable Vision

Perhaps the vision imprinted most memorable

On this late-September, initial visit

To the Inn at Shelbourne Farms,

Was not its graded, grassy lawn-landscape charm

Dotted randomly with fallen crab apple and blown crimson leaf,

Accentuated with the muted-pigment

Of the late-blooming, early-autumn garden

Lined with a gracious tree-wall of various genus

And abundant pointillist color.

Conversely, it was the early-evening illumed half-moon

That dressed the blue-tinted black

Vermont western sky,

Punctuated by a lone-lateral Northern Star

That shown like a diamond

Eminently portrayed as a gift

Cut from some matchless, brilliant nebulae.

Speak

When you disagree with something, speak.

For if you are silent, you will unintentionally be perceived to agree.

Silence is red-hot and not to be golden

When it sends a message never intended.

Of Contrived Intent

It's on thin ice that we skate

When practice to mislead or fabricate;

A lie is a fixture of intended deception

Whose shape and dimension you generally forget;

It's a gamble, a wager, an unwise bet;

For it hangs on the walls of the minds you have duped

Who readily recall the false missives you've spewed

and the lurid basis of your contrived intent;

For when examined and tested will leak like a sieve

Through its foundation of air on which nothing can live;

And yet you'll remain foolishly entrapped in beguiled belief

The staged-life that you lead

Will survive every skeptic

And be forever believed.

On: Profanity

I believe it required

That one's vocabulary be inclusive of words profane;

For if such words did not exist to relieve or sustain

    one's frustration,

I'm willing to bet

That as sure as shit

We'd all be fucking insane.

Gene Pool

A spot,

It forms upon my head,

It grows in silent gender;

It will not stop until it dies

Or hair it once more renders.

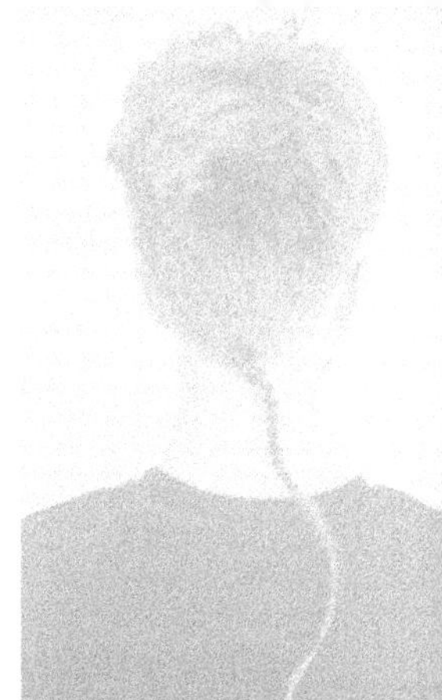

Ode to the Franklin Mills Mall

Rat-tail haircut,

Tattooed arm;

Bare-midriffed tank-top

And a complete lack of charm;

Your wife is pregnant and you still smoke hash,

It's no wonder you're referred to as

Northeast White Trash.

Redeeming Qualities of a Cigar

Redeeming Qualities of a Cigar,

Tobacco leaves soaked in tar;

Rolled-tight, stuck-in mouth and set afire,

Producing smokey stream and billow from this sad and

    incredulous pyre;

Stream and billow infuriate lung and permeates air,

Passersby—noticeably intolerant—grimace and stare.

And when in the company of similar ilk,

Back-slapping smoker—with exuberant pride—

    lifts horrid torch high,

Placed tight in a dual-fingered "V" like some badge of

    accomplishment

To produce an image of what he would like to appear to be.

And when sequestered and on his own

Dismisses any consideration of ever smoking alone,

Placing sole-blame for paying heed to such silly, pretentious

    macho creed

On those unwieldly doses of testosterone.

Ode to Burt's Bees Lip Balm

Through wind that chaps

Or cold that nips;

Scorching sun that dries and gyps;

What rights my lips with loving aplomb?

Why it's my proven tube

Of Burt's Bees Lip Balm.

Coffee that burns when I sip;

Or moisture sapped when I lick,

Or even a nick from my errant Schick,

What heals my lips?

Why it's what you expected all along,

My trusty tube of Burt's Bees Lip Balm.

Whistled notes that sputter or miss;

Spoken words that develop a lisp,

Or when I pucker for that goodnight kiss,

What saves my lips from doing wrong?

It's the one and only Burt's Bees Lip Balm.

A Little Alliteration

Swirling shades of sunlight

Danced deliciously in derelict dress

Upon undressed unsuspecting walls,

While clouds crept cautiously closer

Dictating death, diligently disposing.

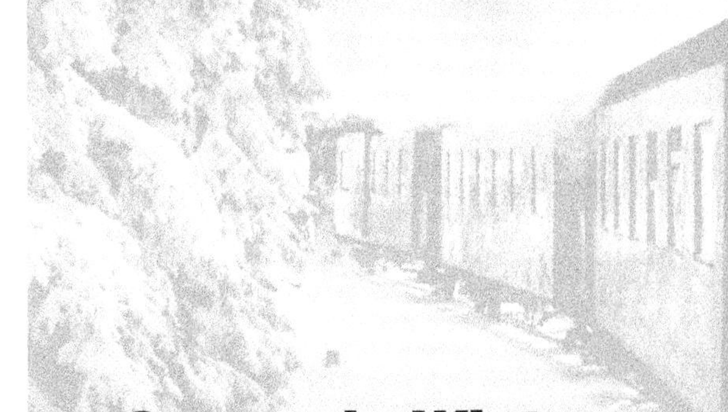

Train Ride at Sunset in Winter

Cold.

Blue-cold. Late December wind:

Blowing steadily from the due-west and north-west,

Invisibly sliding across sidewalk and street through puddle

    and pot-hole;

Careening off curb and hurtling hydrant,

Then scaling up skyline walls and down without tether.

Chilled.

Paled-white skin, iced-blue marrow, sealed in woven-wool coat;

Collar up; head bared and bowed;

Chin pinned against upper chest.

Mindful. Concentrated. Nostrilled exhale pours warm-moist breath

Over lips and chin.

Warm, spilling, downward, sifting through pores of knit-wool

    sweater

and knit cotton-tee, seeping through skin pores to saturate and

reservoir in sternum and breastplate;

Warm, emanating outward to cheek and neck and upper-neck to

    lobe and tip

And then to collar periphery, and then gone.

Coerced.

Nudged and pushed and pulled,

The invisible instigator throttles me;

Pace involuntarily quickened I am dispatched to destined station
    with acceleration–

To catch the late afternoon liner to the City to the North.

So up the avenue past alleys and storefronts and automobiles,

Past citizen and denizen and passerby:

Women in fur coats and fur hats and leathered gloves of tan
    and gold,

In cashmere wraps and velvet hats and high heeled boot;

And men—precariously, incongruously—in parka and ball caps
    and mufflers of chenille,

and leather coats and loafers absent of socks;

All fleeing, all quick-paced, with heads down and collars up;

All obvious, mindful, focused on reaching their destinations from
    the cold.

And the wind-stiffened tails of the neck-wraps of the
    fleeing commuters

exiting the return train from the City to the North, on the aligned
    south track.

Wind, dispatching hats from heads, soaring and tumbling to
    sidewalk and street.

Silence.

Silent, tranquil, yellow-gold sun slopes through

unencumbered winter sky toward linear steel-blue horizon,

Losing its light in the early-winter late afternoon.

Silenced.

Extremities dressed in boot and glove. Numb.

A wiggled toe and a finger snap. Silent. Numb.

I am numb and neutral and complacent on the station platform.

I think of sleep in the silence.

In this stage I produce a silence.

Pale-white eyelids slope toward pink-linear socket.

Faintly, silently, entering my visual periphery, contrasting ground

    shadows of medium-greens and gray-blacks slither and snake

    from street level up cement steps,

Sliding, splaying, skating along the exposed train platform.

Sustained, the invisible frigid wind-current contemporaneously

    shimmies and shakes;

To shake and vibrate the platform of segmented concrete on steel

    beam over frozen ground beneath my feet.

Then, suddenly, gradually gliding into my depth of field a distant

    yellow-white pin-light;

Pale, near-surreal, pierces this early stage of dusk.

Leading, guiding the steel-gray steam engine and rail cars

    that trail;

Moving, curving from rail bridge and from track bend from the

    west and the south;

Visibly, in muffled pitches and creaks and auditory tones,

    speeding, charging toward the landing.

Invisibly, silently, splitting the sea of dense and darkening iced-air;

Fracturing, shattering, now pulverizing the crystallized particles of

    hydrogen and oxygen and remnants of carbon,

Leaving an indignant wake of sifted air.

Now. Train, gradually, relenting, slowing, without sound

approaches the landing.

And even though there is this vibratory disturbance in the pressure

and density of the air,

I hear nothing. Nothing.

All remains silent.

Pin-light, now, fully dilated, fully illuminated now,

Leads locomotive and tethered rail cars past me.

Silently, in an intermittent, jerking, braking pattern,

The steel wheels over steel rails slip and slide to a slow,

slow-motionless stop.

Vibration dissipates without remnant.

Concentrated. Mindful. I exhale a full elongated breath into the

fading near-dusk.

Its pale-white translucence spews out and up,

Contrasting subtly against the variated gray-white silver of the rail

car, it fades, dissipates and is gone.

And the locomotive blocks the setting sun.

Solace.

Car's steel, wire-meshed windowed exterior door glides open

Exposing steep interior steel-stair and dimly-illumed vestibule light.

Passing through door portal. Boarding car. Now, head up and

collar down.

Climbing up-stair I am enveloped by the invisible warm: the

tangency of welcomed tepid heat. Relief from the elements

and the numb.

Passing through interior sliding steel-door portal. Yet
     another portal
of warm, muffled warm, blowing down from overhead duct.
Cascading. Spilling down, down onto exposed head and tip and
     lobe and neck and lower neck;
Seeping through coat fibers and pore of sweater and cotton-tee
to shoulder and shoulder blade and middle back, through skin
     pore to collar-bone and clavicle; collected and sustained in
     sternum and breastplate;
Washing me. Enveloping me. Embracing me.
Solace.
No longer contested and challenged by element and atmosphere;
No longer pushed and pulled by the invisible instigator
I am comforted and warm.
Head up. Looking up-aisle.
Pupils, now, fully dilated in the pale and pinkish fluorescent light,
The product of a million spontaneous collisions
between free electrons and mercury atoms; emanating out,
     tumbling down
from the inner phosphor-coated glass tube affixed to the
     overhead ceiling.
Light, cascading down onto the empty elongated passenger seats
     and occupied seats;
Onto the bared heads and hatted heads and wrapped and
     unwrapped shoulders;
Spilling down and across laps, down pant-leg and bared-leg to
     shoe-top and boot-top

Ultimately trickling to floor; dissipating 'til lost and consumed in—
    ironically, it's self-created shadow.

Fulfilled.

Now. Train, moving, rocking; now, speeding north to the City.

Now. Tired. Collapsing, sinking into soft, worn leather
    cushioned seat.

Now. Looking up and left and west through the ice-white,
gauze-frosted window,

An extraordinary light: the subtle-glare of the yellow-gold stream
    of sun-light;

An interesting and intriguing and inviting light,

Gently piercing the transparent cornea; persuading hazel iris to
    rotate and coil and contract around its black hole portal to
    discern and calculate the absorption of the light.

Light. Now, transiting the crystalline lens bending the light,
    focusing the light through consummate vitreous gel, onto
    macula and then retina: the delicate, light-sensitive membrane
    receiving the light; capturing the light; translating the light;
    inverting the light; conveying the converted light to optic nerve
    and to cerebral cortex and to senses.

To all senses. All senses react.

A million synapses occur and yellow-blue and silver-blue sparks

Spit and fly from the chain of nerve impulses.

And I am intrigued and fulfilled as I react to the Sun:
    the now tiring Sun.

Now, languishing out and over and across linear cobalt-
    blue horizon;

Collapsing. Now sinking. Now exhaling its final linear

    gold-yellow breath;

Spilling down, pouring over around and through the silhouetted

    string of stark leafless trees frozen in the foreground.

The Trees: all interspersed and entwined.

All with splintered twig and cracked and faulted branch and

    textured bark

and creviced limb.

And The Light. The final light: conjoined with train speeding to

    final northern landing.

Together, collaborating, producing the rapid scenic staccato

    glint-and-flicker of the slumbering sun through the

    silhouetted fractures;

Impeccably paralleled and in unison with the interspersed

    cadence of clatter and thrum, clatter and thrum of the steel

    wheels meeting the steel rails

Of this train ride at sunset in winter.

Side Street of Home

I think I'll retire and retire to Nome,

With ashtray and keyboard and memoir of home,

Where life's predilections

Were nurtured alone

In front yard and backyard

And side street of home.

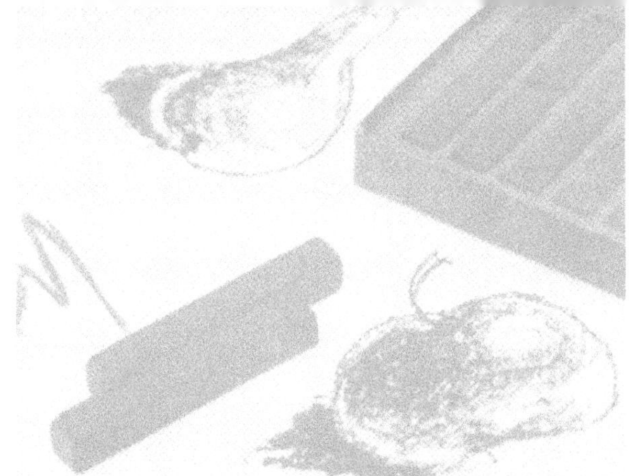

A Touch of Immortality

Charcoal drawings on the floor;
Poems written, there will be more.
The smell of oil paint from the room down the hall;
Scattered cartoons affixed to a wall.
Short stories cemented to a once blank page;
A sketchbook grows yellow with undying age.
Parts of my life have been left in many places,
Perhaps to be witnessed by the ageless faces;
Maybe they'll remember me, and then again not,
For it's more for the art than the legacy
Than one should ever want.

Thoughts and Observations

(Man is the only animal
that jots things down.)

Never give an eraser to a cartoon character with suicidal tendencies.

৶

I wonder what a merry-go-round sounds like in an echo chamber.

৶

No man is an island, but he who lisps is an isthmus.

৶

Rhetoric is when a mortician gives you his business card.

৶

A troublemaker is not the culprit, but rather, the instigator of reaction.

৶

People never change. They shower every once in a while, but they never change.

৶

No one's perfect; yet, everyone's a critic.

৶

And just what do you get for the man who has
everything? Penicillin.

It's what people think they know that concerns me, not
what they actually know.

If you really want to get to know someone, just watch
them eat.

Love is the consistent, unconditional respect for the
mind, the body, and the heart.

Romance is a slow and unhurried and
meaningful act, perfect and unspoiled in its
purpose and everlasting if right.

Love is a time, a moment, a duration; a path, a
way, a direction; a vision, a specter, an image;
confusion, transition, solitude; a place, a dimension,
a marriage; a life.

When I am with others, I would rather be alone, and
when I'm with you, I never want to be alone again.

⁓

I fell for you when we first met, and I have yet to land.

⁓

Love's only requirements are honesty and communication.

⁓

Love is a series of unselfish acts which require no
effort or conscience.

⁓

Love can be felt either in touched thought or
untouched hand.

⁓

Love is an emotion that fine-tunes and enhances
all the others.

⁓

Sex is a moments time in a day, whereas love can
derive a day from a moments time.

⁓

And you are like a deep breath, to be held for just so many heartbeats, then exhaled and returned to the wind.

෧

If variety is the spice of life, then love must certainly be its nourishment.

෧

We are nothing until accepted, and empty until fulfilled by another.

෧

We may need food and water to survive, but it is emotion that sustains us.

෧

Emotion is like the fragile egg. If you play with it and disrespect it, it will break. But, if you nurture and honor it, it will flourish and give life.

෧

Opposites may attract, but once the differences are realized the magnetism generally wears off.

෧

It's not love that makes the world go around,
it's revolving credit.

ᴄ᷍ᴏ

You cannot produce happiness and you cannot
control despair.

ᴄ᷍ᴏ

The act of procreation not only creates a new life;
it also directly and indirectly effects and alters every
other life that exists.

ᴄ᷍ᴏ

Gossip is that grassroots groundswell, perpetrated by
whispers and allusions, and perpetually sustained by
nothing more than more of the same.

ᴄ᷍ᴏ

A secret is a curiously contrived and circuitous tale that
everyone can't wait to tell, yet compels the recipient to
never utter a word of it to anyone else.

ᴄ᷍ᴏ

The benefit of taking the bus is that you get to meet people you would never let in your car.

❧

There are three times in your life when you are "blessed": When you're born, when you die, and when you sneeze.

❧

Age is not the enemy, but rather, the complacent adversary of youth.

❧

I may age, but I will never be old.

❧

The upside to thinning hair is that it's so much easier to keep every single one of them in place.

❧

A bald spot is nothing more than a glaring deficiency.

❧

It always seems I have been older than younger. The
thought of youth always just a breath away, yet never to
be inhaled again.

⁂

We are neither young nor old, merely entities with
futures and memories.

⁂

Time does not fly, it evaporates.

⁂

Time is the basic form of suicide; it continually
eliminates itself.

⁂

The clock is everyone's personal, silent,
numerical dictator.

⁂

Time is a healer to the patient; an affliction to
the anxious.

⁂

Time is not a measure; but rather, a continual
predecessor to itself.

❧

For me, perfect symmetry is to die on your
birthday of natural causes and to be awarded
a Certificate of Completion.

❧

There will always be tomorrow, but there will never be
today again.

❧

A humorist will make you think before you laugh;
a comedian will make you laugh before you think.

❧

After spending an entire weeknight evening maligned in
the comatose behavior of viewing consecutive, prime-
time network television shows, I am
thoroughly convinced that people who have accepted
such barren, banal behavior as intrinsic and
compulsory are the same constituents of this society
who are equally compelled to kill an entire weekend
methodically arranging stuffed animal menageries in the
rear window of the family sedan.

❧

And just how "current" could a paleontologist ever be?!

An explanation is something a man will give a woman
far more often than he will flowers.

When a guy is single, he goes to a bar to entice women.
And when married, goes there to complain about them.

There is nothing worse than a bartender who doesn't
have peripheral vision.

People that are tested for inebriation should not be
forced to take a breathalyzer or give blood. Instead, they
should be asked to simply repeat "I am an enigma" one
time fast.

If drinking and driving is illegal, why do bars
have parking lots?

After drinking alcohol through a straw, I decided that "fuel injection" has nothing to do with automobile engines.

❧

There are those that honor their bodies as temples; whereas, I treat mine more like a health club affiliated with a sports bar and restaurant.

❧

If Jackson Pollock or Salvadore Dali made you a drink, just what the heck would it look like, and how would you actually drink it?

❧

Perhaps the only thing you can give away, that you do not own, is a barstool.

❧

Golf is that gentlemanly endeavor that provides the participants 18 holes in which to perfect the fine art of profanity.

❧

Golf isn't a game; it's a character builder.

☙

Honesty is always the best policy. Unless it's golf.

☙

Maturity is the ability to understand and accept "no" and
to appreciate and respect "yes."

☙

Curiosity is the perfect portal to a sustained youth.

☙

Perhaps the most effective way to deal with a child's end-
less queries and redundant observations is to
forever keep them ignorant of speech.

☙

Kids are good for two things: tax purposes and old age.

☙

A child's worst enemy is gravity.

☙

To a kid, food is a toy they can eat.

⁓

I wonder how amoebas handle schizophrenia.

⁓

I wonder if an amoeba is capable of granting its
undivided attention.

⁓

I am genuinely ambivalent about my indecisiveness.

⁓

A hobby is something you enjoy that doesn't
necessarily require a high degree of skill. Whereas,
a profession is something you don't necessarily enjoy of
which skill is a requisite.

⁓

Boredom is generally stimulated by absolutely nothing.

⁓

An "idle conversation" is one that never quite gets
into gear.

⁓

Laziness is the ability to do absolutely nothing at a
moment's notice.

&

Ambiguity is the gerrymander of a definition.

&

Paranoia is when you're at a football game and you think
the guys in the huddle are talking about you.

&

To get to Carnegie Hall I didn't "practice, practice, prac-
tice," I took a cab.

&

Fantasies are generally devoid of imperfection
because they lack a third dimension. You need depth
to create imperfection.

&

For some the brain is a constant companion, and, for
others, it's a stranger that never comes to visit.

&

I think it's okay to lose your mind every once in
a while, just as long as you are not suffering from
amnesia at the time.

৩

Your brain can either be your best friend
or your worst enemy.

৩

The easiest way to invite trouble is to allow your mouth
to be just a step ahead of your brain.

৩

When you think that you have all the answers, you
should probably give it a little more thought.

৩

If anything, it is the confusion in our lives that is most
welcome; it's the perfect distraction to everything else.

৩

Confusion is a good thing because, at the very least,
it keeps your mind occupied.

৩

We think, we wonder, we question; We relate, we
realize, we answer; We equate, we conform, we relax;
We are.

⁂

To remember, you must think; to think, you must
understand; to understand, you must care; to care,
you must feel; and to feel, you must truly be alive.

⁂

Perspective is that element of life that runs when
we try to touch it, and begs for comfort when we
try to ignore it.

⁂

Ignorance is nothing more than voluntary stupidity.

⁂

Ignorance has never done anyone any favors.

⁂

Ignorance never gets you anywhere;
it just keeps you where you are.

⁂

The thought of knowledge is a dream; the knowledge of thought, a tangible.

*

Leaving nothing to chance is providing a member of the automobile club a place in your funeral procession.

*

I think it ironic that the "humane" society is for the benefit of animals.

*

Hearing is a sense; listening an art.

*

If someone tells you to shut up, it must be that they're listening to what you have to say.

*

Problems are nothing if they make sense.

*

A copycat is the original's protégé.

&

You must be aware of what you have before you
complain about what's missing.

&

To avoid disappointment, you must also avoid
expectation.

&

It seems we are never bored by nature. Perhaps that is
why we escape to it rather than from it.

&

In nature there is no waste; everything is consumed,
recycled, and returned for a purpose.

&

An argument is a discussion generally devoid
of communication.

&

You never know what you are going
to hear until you listen.

§

Don't keep your thoughts to yourself, for expressing your-
self is man's dire need to seed the thoughts of others.

§

When you "fly by the seat of your pants," you may not be
airborne for long, but the fact that you got off the ground
at all is probably a victory unto itself.

§

At a time when we, as civilized people, should be
sharpening our communication skills to enhance
and ensure a peaceful and sustained coexistence
with our fellow man, it appears that the overabundant
and intimidating supply, coupled with the cavalier
and reactionary use of firearms to mediate the
most innocent of confrontations, will certainly
preclude many from ever exercising that initial and
honest endeavor.

§

Democracy is voting your conscience,
even if it isn't on the ballot.

၏

How does anyone disagree with fiction? It doesn't exist!

၏

Recent government studies show that 95 percent of
the people that take generic drugs have been proven
to lack any form of identity.

၏

Ever hear the one about the kleptomaniac that got
robbed, and didn't know it?

၏

Ever hear the one about the pyromaniac who suffered
from kleptomania? Yeah, he wound up starting the
fire with stolen matches.

၏

Man is the only animal that jots things down.

၏

The more you experience, the more you have to
fall back on.

❧

The thing about the unexpected is we never anticipate it
because it is never welcome. The error being it will have
no relevance until it happens.

❧

For those that know me, no explanation is necessary, and
for those who do not, no explanation will suffice.

❧

A writer's purpose is to reflect behavior using words
as his mirror and syntax his armor.

❧

There is no answer until there is no question left.

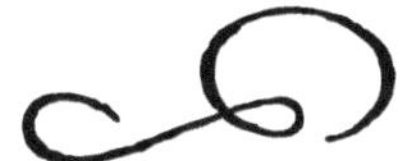

Sketches

The Leaf App

I have absolutely no trees on my property.

However, every Autumn, said yard is summarily smothered in dried, decaying leaves. And just how the heck did that happen?

Simple. They're someone else's leaves. Plain and simple. So, I was figuring, since they're not technically "mine," why can't I just return every single one of them to their rightful owner?

And just how the heck would I ever be able to possibly do that in an efficient, accurate, and unbiased way? you ask.

Simple! I give you the *Leaf App*, which I have just developed. Still a prototype, I proffer; however, based on a recent round of promising presentations, discussions, and progressive nego-tiations, I think I'm pretty darn close to a legitimate patent and licensing deal with the National Arbor Day Foundation. I know. I never knew they existed either. Huh. Lucky me.

Said *Leaf App* is designed to identify the specific neighbor's tree(s), corresponding leaves, and how they found their way into your yard. The way this works is: Once downloaded to your smart phone or device, you scan the leaf to the app where it timestamps, analyzes and defines the species, origin, duration and direction of flight, and length of time on your lawn. And it's quite efficient and accurate. When using the universally accept-ed metric for leaf volume calculation, "Wheelbarrow Capacity," approximately 350 to 550 leaves can be scanned on a single "air-swipe" of the phone. And, once downloading the data to my AI-generated, state-of-the-art garden rake (patent pending), when combing the specifically sensored rake-prongs through a mixed smattering of itinerant leaves, separation by identity, tree of origin, and property address are summarily recorded on the app, supported by a printout receipt (just in case any of this stuff winds up in court).

I believe that once the thousands of leaves that I have conscientiously raked, identified, and returned to their proper owners, the neighborhood, as a whole will be much better for it. "A place for everything and everything in its place," as my mother liked to say. She also used to say, "Cleanliness is next to Godliness." It's a stretch, but I don't think that really applies here.

And I do realize and expect there may be initial shock, perhaps varying degrees of incredulity, intransigence, or even outright blowback from the neighbors once they see their leaves "returned." But I am prepared. Luckily for me—once again, the National Arbor Day Foundation saw this coming. So, to appease said victims and to provide an assuring sense of equanimity and acceptance, it curiously offers a market-tested, subscription-free TikTok sensitivity training podcast hosted by a newly minted, really fast-talking transcendental arborist and recently disbarred yoga instructor who's wanted in three states and the District of Columbia. Oh. I'm sure that'll be just fine. Yeah. That oughta work.

Consider the Source

There is a rather rational saying that urges us to "mind our own business." Easy enough for some, I would suspect, however, for others it is a compulsion that must be exercised with unhindered frequency, undeniable assurance, and unquestioned correctness in order to sustain their penchant to ultimately help save others from themselves. You would think that these self-imposed saviors of mankind would probably have enough of their own fractures, fissions, and flaws to fix and fiddle with to keep them sufficiently occupied and out of our lives. But this is precisely what makes their pompous probes, uninvited opinions, and unwelcome advice so curiously ironic and hypocritical. For example: the first one that comes to mind is the chain-smoker who lectures the sun-worshipper on the evils of skin cancer. That's a good one. Or, the athletically inept sports talk show host offering strategy to the slumping superstar. The guilty-as-charged, sex-offending pulpit preacher saving his flock from sin. The congressionally censured senior statesman providing ethical direction to a confused constituent. And others, like the twice-divorced marriage counselor or the previously incarcerated corrections officer, and, a favorite, the pontificating, pilfering charity chairman. Admittedly, some advice is honorable and often applicable; however, before acceptance and practice it is probably best that we first procure another rational saying, "Consider the source."

Concentrate

The concept of being a smart person (regarding the ability to conjure up a fact at a moment's notice) is based on the idea that you have the ability to forget to forget. I know you're probably not following me. I shall illustrate. You see, if you remember to forget then you will. Forget, that is. And, if you forget to forget, then you will remember, because you forgot to forget what you were supposed to remember in the first place. Damn. That was easy.

Cliché

There is an adage that invites us to "think before we speak." Too often we all are guilty of not adhering to this nugget of advice, especially when it comes to our senseless, involuntary—even lazy—utterances, where we string words to formulate certain verbal syntax, known adroitly as "The Cliché." For example, often it is in the form of a prelude to the body of a sentence: "I was thinking to myself..." And just who else would you be thinking to? "If I do say so myself..." A bit elite, and definitely redundant. "I, personally myself..." You mean, You?! Or, as a stand-alone, innocuous, insipid sentence: "Be that as it may." What?! Or, as unintended pleadings: "I beg your pardon." Alright, then get on your knees and beg for it! "Can you please hold?" (the phone) Yeah. Sure. I'll get a good grip. "May I have your name?" Okay. But just for a while 'cuz I'm really gonna need it this afternoon. Futile decrees: "Watch your mouth!" I tried that once and I damn-near went cross-eyed. "Watch what you say!" Nope. Can't be done. Repugnant rumination: "You took the words right out of my mouth." Yeccch. "It was right on the tip of my tongue." And you swallowed it, right?! Cerebral concessions: "I haven't the foggiest." Unfortunately, that's your only weather pattern. "I can't make heads or tails." And it probably wouldn't matter. Yup. Clichés are indeed overused, commonplace, uninteresting, and unoriginal. And, sadly, this is probably why we're so comfortable with them.

A Real Eye Opener

I was little concerned, to say the least, when I made my initial visit to meet my new eye doctor. The music wafting from the inter-office sound system filled the dimly-lit waiting room with the strains of Stevie Wonder, Ray Charles, and Jose Feliciano. The good doctor came tripping in sporting a pair of very thick, dark sunglasses, clutching and tapping a long pencil-thin cane, and was accompanied by a leashed-canine not to be mistaken for a German shepherd. Innately aware of the subtle shock and distinct concern etched on my face that he may be sightless, he attempted to put me at ease by explaining that this escapade was merely a practical joke, solely for my benefit and to fulfill his droll penchant for levity. That being said, any possibility of attaining a comfort level with this guy was quickly dashed when the dear optometrist turned on his heel, tripped over the cane, stumbled face forward and summarily exited head over heels through his second story office window.

Your Time or Your Life

People like to characterize time as something that "flies."

I always counter that it merely "evaporates."

But if you think about the totality and dimension and circumference of time, it is integrated into more than just flying and evaporating.

For instance, it is also absorbed. Absorbed in the sense that if I had not taken and integrated the time to achieve that goal, it would have never succeeded. The absorption of time melded into the thought and infrastructure of an accomplishment; any accomplishment is indispensable.

Time may also be reflected in composing the rhyme, meter, and conclusion of a poem or a conversation or a thought that you never had before and now realize that it qualifies as an actual, legitimate epiphany. Perhaps your first!

And then that essence of time that is "invested" or "earmarked" or, strangely, "lost."

That being its conscious allocation, appointed designation, or ultimately, woefully, it is squandered or neglected.

And time is not just a general concept; it's more a specific element. An element deemed more valuable and indispensable than, perhaps, money; cold, hard cash;

mammon, that "root of all evil." It would be the new currency; the new commodity. So valuable that one could be held up, in broad daylight on a pedestrian laden street, for their time. "Hey! Buddy! Stick 'em up. Your time or your life!"

OK. But how much of my time do you want?

"I figure eight years oughta do it."

"Eight? Why eight?"

"Time served for tax evasion. But they let me out early when they deemed money no longer useful or usable."

"That was you? I remember that."

"Plus, I'm sixty-six, and I'd really like to meet my calculated actuarial life table age limit of seventy-four. Call me greedy."

"Well. I'm only thirty, and with a promising career and a fledgling family. There must be other options. Why don't you pick on a retiree? They have nothing but time. They wouldn't put up a stink, and they'd probably hand it over without even blinking an eye. I've seen retirees. They never blink."

"Sounds good! You're off the hook."

Greg. The Vicarious Champion

I used to work with this guy who clerked in the office file room. Every Friday during football season he would wear his favorite team's jersey to the office to show his allegiance, support, and self-importance to the success of the team's performance for that coming Sunday. And he would, in devout seriousness and unequivocal belief, tell you that he, Greg from the file room, was integral to the team's success. And he would pull me aside to tell me—emphatically, that "we have a real good team this year." Realizing that his obsequious zeal and deluded importance to a professional football team's games outcome—and overall success for the season, ultimately hinged on a file room clerk in New Jersey, I wanted to give him some relevance and perspective. I said, "No, Greg. 'They' have a good team. You're, you know, just a fan."

And when they lost, he would call in sick. Returning a day or two later, he'd show up despondent and dazed. We sort of worried about him. But not to the point of total concern because, after all, this was his fantasy, and none of us wanted to be sucked into Greg's den of delusion. I mean, if he did something dramatic, like threaten to jump from a bridge or something, I'm sure the office consensus would be, "Sure. Yeah. Okay, Greg. Go ahead."

And then, when his team did win the Super Bowl, we cringed. For we knew what we may be in for.

And sure enough, that "Super Bowl Monday," Greg was in full favorite-football-team regalia, right down to those black paint-like smears under his eyes that only the players should actually require. Then, as I was passing the file room, he emerged, pumping his fist in the air and pronouncing in ultimate declaration, "We Won! We Won!!" And I said, emphatically, "No, Greg. They Played! They Won! You WATCHED! Geez! Get a grip, for crying out loud."

Unfazed, he grabbed his faux Super Bowl Trophy, held it high above his head, and proceeded to strut victoriously around the office.

Know Your Audience

We seldom have house guests. Maybe once or twice a year.

So, for the most part, I give very little thought to my morning routine. It consists of, with few modifications or considerations, a bowl of fruit—favorably peeled and sectioned clementines—a dollop of a verified Greek yogurt, sprinkled with a half-dozen blueberries, and a small glass of fat-free milk. Then, after a respite, a sliced Thomas' English raisin muffin; toasted, and generously spread with an Irish butter that my wife got me, which I watch melt to perfection, consummated with a generous thermos of coffee.

That's it. Nearly every day. Yes, dear reader, I am a creature of habit. And you could put that on my gravestone. But please don't, I'm to be cremated.

So, we had this rare family visit: my wife's cousin and his new bride. Nice enough people. He's quite bookish and laid back; she more of the fastidious, 'everything in its place' type. Showed them every courtesy and hospitality upon their arrival. A fine bed and private bath; the now required and applicable password and router access to a secure internet, and anything else they may need or require. Pretty straightforward; pretty simple.

Now, I'm generally up in the morning before most—another one of those habits I'll never break or tire of, anticipating my scheduled breakfast.

So, having finished my fruit and milk, sticking to my routine as I plopped the two halves of my English muffin into the 4-slice capacity toaster, my cousin's new wife appears in the kitchen. While exchanging the socially scripted "Good mornings" and—what I never understood, "How did you sleep?" queries, my muffins popped-up from the toaster. Making it her business, she studies the placement of the two halves at opposite ends of the four available slots.

Knowing she is a stickler for order and reason, I grimace, palpably aware of her intransigence to such a thing.

"That's not right! Why do you put your toast in opposite ends of the toaster?" she demands.

"Oh. Just to raise suspicion and confusion; doubt and inquiry," I respond, as I ply the butter, watch it melt, and move on to another room.

"The Assignment" (A Literal Interpretation)

Whilst a high school teenager I got my first, real, authentic girl-friend. New to love, I told her I'd do anything to be with her. Anything. Then one day my mouth got way out in front of my brain, and before I realized it, I had said something really dumb about her hair or clothes or nails or something. Heck. I really don't remember. I really don't. Attempting to quickly mend the gaff, she beat me to it and told me, "Why don't you go fuck yourself." I know. You're right. I didn't know how I was going to do it, either. I mean, it sounds so unimaginably, physiologically inconceivable. Just trying to picture it made my hamstrings cramp up. But I knew she really meant it. The full, unemotional, almost vapid eye contact, and phrased so calmly and coldly, any form of punctuation wasn't even a consideration. I figured that such a terse response—and obscure request—should at least garner an exclamation point or something, for crying out loud. So, under-standing the full weight of her rather suggestive directive, and recalling that I had promised her I would do "anything" to be with her, I decided to well, you know, go "F" myself.

Again, being new to this whole love thing and girlfriends that make certain inhumanly possible demands, and having never consummated up to that point—not even sort of, barely knowing actually how to accomplish such a deed—I needed to seek ad-vice on how to you know "bring about" such a physical anomaly. Heck. My father blushed at bra commercials, so I knew he was out. I considered the gym teacher in 8th grade that "taught" sex-ed. We young lads didn't give it a full "education" endorsement because the extent of his "syllabus" was a single - sort of covert and quickly arranged - boys-only Monday night meeting, held in the school cafeteria with our fathers in tow. We watched a film strip comprised of male and female silhouettes with arrows depicting the location of certain genitalia (cumbersome, suggestive positioning of said silhouettes) accompanied by the gym teacher's nervously presented voice over, followed by a quick Q&A and an awkward, silent, single-file exit of the participants from said lunchroom. So, he was out.

Next, I thought maybe the biology teacher. But I was just a freshman and biology wasn't on the learning curriculum for another year. Plus, the teacher, Miss Peacock, was rumored to be in a relationship with Miss Kelly the guidance counselor. So, as confused and perplexed as I was about the task that was already in front of me, I really didn't want to add to the sum of the moving parts already on my plate. If you know what I mean.

I next considered the school's newly appointed, head librarian. Compared to the austere, spinster-type relic she had replaced, she was younger and cooler and seemed somewhat comfortably approachable. Plus, she being a student of arts and letters, according to the framed masters diploma hanging on the wall behind the library counter, perhaps, somewhere in her studies she may have come across something slightly akin to my self-imposed assignment and, if so, any known, recorded history of resolve to such an unorthodox concept and any actual instructive literature to back it up.

So, eyeing and planning the right moment, I discretely placed myself at the unoccupied end of the library's rather lengthy front counter and furtively motioned for her to come join me. Nervously, awkwardly, demonstrably, I shamefully shared with her, at some considerable length and detail, my precarious plight and unique, self-inflicted assignment. Upon divulging the discounting of my father, the 8th grade gym coach, and the biology teacher as reasonable sources of resolve, I paused, swallowed hard, and requested her advice and guidance for how to actually accomplish such a deed, and to, you know, "pull off" such an anatomic abnormality.

Quietly digesting my rather formidable situation, she paused, slowly tapping her long, finely manicured finger nails on the counter. Finally, she looked me in the eye and said knowingly, "I can help you."

"You can?!" I gushed in relief.

"Yup. I have heard of this before, and with very similar circumstances to you." She said it was unique, rare even, but not unprecedented. While she was a graduate school student studying an elective on ancient Hindu religious, cultural, and philosophical writings concerning social hierarchies, gender roles, and power dynamics, she had come across a similar young man's quandary in a case study in Europe. She added that the Europeans are so much more advanced in such things than us priggish Americans. Thank God for the Europeans, I thought to myself. She went on to tell me that his cure was through the study of Kama Sutra. "You know," she said, "that ancient Indian Hindu treatise, so-called the 'Book of Love' on human sexual behavior. Have you ever heard of this book?" Geez. Are you kidding! Not only had I heard of this sexually suggestive directive, I had actually read it! You see, my knowledge of this particular "reference book" was acquired rather haphazardly, yet quite innocently. When I was about twelve or thirteen, I found my older brother in my parent's walk-in closet leafing through the dog-eared copy that my father probably thought no one would ever find buried beneath a stack of old *Sports Illustrateds.* Vividly recalling its explicit content, it was more than just a "Book of Love," it was more of a "how to" on, well, you know, how to! Replete with incredibly suggestive illustrations of the perfectly proportioned carnal contortionist body positions of the male and female participants, no less—and the descriptive captions, ancillary write-ups, and fortuitous footnotes providing numbered steps and placement rules for seeking sexual and sensuous and sensual pleasure in accordance with this particular philosophy. It sure gave me a whole new meaning to the adage "It takes two to tango."

Sharing this revelation with her, she decided it was okay to give me the upshot on the generalities of the study, its basic thesis, and aftermath. As she recalled, it was mostly full of rhetoric and generalities. She unabashedly skirted the details, how he ultimately performed the requested feat, then shared it with his girlfriend, who took him back. The Librarian didn't recall any particular details on the available positions that he may have used to reach his moment of well, you know, "accomplishment" shall we say. "Not a particular guideline," she mused, "but if this helps, I vividly recall the appendix suggesting something that is more 'knees and elbows' required than 'shoulders and spines;' a forewarning to have a game plan, and to not just 'wing it." Reading my reactive furrowed and curious countenance, she then left. Her swift return revealed a retrieved dust covered, truncated, sort of "Cliffs Notes" version of this ancient Hindu Sanskrit study she had unearthed from the library's cryptic catacombs during her initial orientation, led by, interestingly enough, her austere predecessor. Hmmm. Maybe not so much the "spinster-type relic" after all? I thought to myself.

Handing it to me, she cautioned it was not the purported toxic sex manual people grossly misrepresented it to be, but rather, a "broader explanation of human desire, love, and the pursuit of pleasure." Normally, she counseled with an eye twinkle, "two may be better than one, but remember, you'll be flying solo."

Well sir. I must tell you, emulating that Kama Sutra stuff sure was a wake-up call to one's dexterity, flexibility, and those mind-over-matter skills and limits. I'm athletic, but this was stuff way beyond those gym class physical fitness tests. Heck. Greco-Roman Wrestling, breakdancing, even being double-jointed wouldn't hold a candle. So, after the twisting and turning and contorting and torquing and contusing and concussing, and bruising and blood-letting—well not bloodletting but, to be honest, there was that potential—I did not, in fact, "expletive" myself. 10th Grade biology would confirm that.

Then, upon my release from the Emergency Ward, the team of surgeons and physio experts that had hastily gathered to attend to my various muscle pulls and ligament tears and glaring contusions, advised that after all that I had put myself through, they kinda wished that I had, in fact, accomplished the act. For, it would have afforded them the desired and esteemed authorship of not only medical journal-type publications and important academic-related papers but, perhaps, more importantly, an un-paralleled repository of some really, really fantastic stories, clever asides, and humorous anecdotes to offer up and even brag about at important dinner parties and professional conferences for the rest of their natural lives!

And, although I had failed to achieve my girlfriend's direct and specific command, after hearing of my dedication and sacrificial exploits to retain her love, she took me back, saying how im-pressed she was, and promising to "show me" that it was "defi-nitely worth the effort." Needless to say, I was more than relieved that she said that, when she could have said, "If at first you don't succeed...try, try again." Ouch!

Time in Memorial

Nearly out of time, I did double-time and worked overtime to find the time to borrow the time to buy the time to invest the time to earn the time to make more time. Then with time on my hands, not valuing time, I lost the time by spending the time and wasting the time on just having a good 'ol time. So, out of time, I stole some time and did some time. Having served my time, I was granted time to create the time to save the time to allot the time to manage the time to consider the time before my time is up.

You Know You're Getting Older When...

When you learn that your neighbor's parents are
younger than you are.

When your two new favorite rooms in the house are the
upstairs bathroom and the downstairs bathroom.

When someone asks what "streaming service"
you use, and you give them the name and phone
number of your urologist.

When asked if you're on Instagram, you say you haven't
been on a diet plan in years.

When you would rather just look at your toes than
actually try to touch them.

When trying to be hip, you phone an Uber (whatever
that is) to get a ride to the app store (wherever that is).

When you pull something just by scratching
something else.

When you realize "be still my heart" should no longer be
one of your go-to clichés.

When your knee brace and cane actually qualify as
fashion accessories.

When passersby yell, "Hey! Nice wheels!" they're talking
about your walker.

When your blood pressure is tied directly to the
number of times you hear a Millennial trying to
squeeze the word "like" into a single sentence.

When you're referred to as a "museum piece" for reading
a newspaper on a front porch.

When you diligently adhere to the posted speed limit
and contentedly stay in the far, right-hand lane.

When told you must wear a bicycle helmet,
you advise the instigator that you managed to survive
childhood without one.

When you're the only one in the room who
still ties their shoelaces.

When you grow comfortable with the fact that hair is
an element that grows on your back, under your arms,
between your legs, over your eyes and in your ears, but
not on top of your head.

When your barber absolutely insists on trimming your
eyebrows.

When at restaurants, you'd rather starve than download
the menu app.

When at dinner parties, you overhear someone
float the names of your dermatologist and heart
specialist to complete strangers.

When you have to flip-on the heating pad just to
make it to happy hour.

When you now bar "walk."

When you learn that the Smithsonian has just added a
phone booth to its permanent collection.

When someone mentions "AI" you think it's
something about a shooting guard who used to play
for the Philadelphia 76ers.

When you bend over to pick something up and wonder
how something could fall that far that fast.

When your physical therapist now qualifies as an official
member of your extended family.

When the TV movie is in a foreign language—with
subtitles—and you still insist on turning up the volume.

Whenever someone says the word "libido," you confuse
it with that 70's pop hit dance tune by Boz Skaggs.

When your new, all-time favorite go-to word in Scrabble
is "ibuprofen."

When you've been diagnosed with all those things that
you remember your grandparents talking about.

When talking in your sleep you confirm the television careers of Howard Duff and Ida Lapino.

When the only time you think about sex is when required to check that certain box on a new patient medical questionnaire.

When your great-nephew is graying at the temples and smokes a pipe.

When that song you can't get out of your head you probably first heard on an 8-Track tape.

When you consider yourself a "night owl" when not in bed by nine.

When you smile, it could be gas.

When you know what room you're in, but not quite sure
what suddenly compelled you to be there.

When your back and knees start reminding you to never
do that again.

When growing up, your parents never hired anyone to
clean the house or cut the grass.

When things you "never gave a thought to" you now
can't stop thinking about.

When AARP starts sending you birthday cards.

When someone says it's "to die for" you quickly ask if
there would be another reason for doing it.

When you learn that you've been nominated for a "Lifetime Achievement Award."

When you're the only one on your block that still uses a push mower and a rake.

When staring at a QR Code, all you see is that ink-blot test that kept you out of the Army.

When the same countries you knew as a kid are still at War.

When you've just outlived your third dog.

When that kitten you just got will probably out-live you.

When providing your date of birth, the recipient responds with, "Oh. Wow. Good for you!"

When that 25th year reunion was fifteen years ago.

When the shopping cart now doubles as a walker.

When your "bucket list" now includes coming off the meds and returning the catheter.

When ID'd for a liquor purchase, you tell the proprietor this is the 45th anniversary of your 21st birthday.

When your doctor ends every prognosis with the refrain, "Medicare'll probably cover that."

When losing your teeth and hearing are accepted as reasonable rites of passage.

When you see your pharmacist more often than members of your immediate family.

When the toys you played with as a kid show up on
consecutive episodes of *Antiques Roadshow.*

When your telephone suddenly became better
known as a "landline."

When you inform a gathering that you're "pushing 60,"
and you get absolutely no pushback.

When the plaque they have named for you provides
available space for the word "memorial."

When the last time someone referred to you
as a "senior," you were just about to graduate
from something.

When for Halloween you go as a
social security recipient.

When your heart specialist tells your wife, "Remember. No surprise parties."

When the age spots on the back of your hand start to mimic a certain constellation.

When that "'til death do us part us part" vow starts getting your attention.

When the hue of your toenails starts to match the mustard stains on your sweatpants.

When you start waiving the "lifetime warranty" option on stuff.

When that "gets better with age" axiom doesn't necessarily apply to everything.

When your doctor suggests a battery of tests before
giving you the green light for "taking a hot tub."

When you attend a reunion and find yourself surrounded
by nothing but old people.

When you make a fist for your doctor, and he says, "I
said make a fist."

When you hear of something "going viral," you choose to
not get involved for personal health and safety reasons.

When you're the only one in the office that still drinks
tap water.

When you wear a wristwatch that only tells
you the time.

When approaching a flight of stairs, people
suddenly come out of nowhere to guide you by
the elbow and forearm.

When "timing is everything" starts to conjoin with
unscheduled bodily functions.

When asked if you need any help, you say,
"Oh. All I can get."

When you remember being able to buy anything without
something called a "promo code."

When you first saw the recent Hall of Fame inductee
play as a minor leaguer.

When your favorite topics of conversation are a
recent dental implant and a series of jokes you heard
at the senior center.

When asked to supervise a toddler, you realize that you're the one who should probably be watched.

When trying to finish your meal, and the waitress wants to know if you're "still workin'?" you sarcastically offer, "No. I've actually been retired for the past six years."

When you find yourself saying stuff like, "When I was your age!" while wildly waving your right index finger.

When, in mixed company, you realize you're the only one that still remembers telephone numbers.

When you're suddenly your parents' age.

When you are quite sure that you have never "wrapped your head" around anything.

When a hearty laugh is just enough to send you
scrambling for your inhaler.

When your kneecaps begin to dimple.

When "bruises easily" is no longer just a metaphor.

When the only "jogging" you do these days is when
testing your memory.

When just ripping off a Band Aid results in a trip to
the ER for stitches.

When ordering a "regular" coffee at Starbucks, people
stare at you and the room goes silent.

When you put your proctologist on speed-dial.

When just getting out of bed qualifies as "multitasking."

When you start wearing suspenders - with a belt!

When your last outdoor rock concert was before they
had Ticketmaster.

When loved ones start peppering you with questions
about the legal status of your "last will and testament."

When you solicit a parish priest to teach you Latin
so you can properly pronounce all of your
medical conditions.

When "SPAM" went from being known as a tasty, canned
luncheon meat to a barrage of unsolicited emails.

When your "train of thought" has left the station, but struggles to make the roundtrip.

When certain food groups are no longer best friends with your colon.

When procrastination becomes less and less voluntary.

When all your contemporaries start "downsizing."

When that "podcast" thing used to be simply known as a "radio show."

When you can still think of everything, just not at the right time or in the right order.

When your grab-bag gift at a retiree's send-off includes an application for "meals on wheels."

When you just experienced something for the third time that was supposed to be "once in a lifetime."

When you suddenly want to take an English Composition refresher course to ensure that your "last words" are grammatically correct.

When you were five-foot-eleven, but now you're five-foot-ten.".

When peering in the mirror, you find it best to respect the changes than to argue with the past.

When the last thing you said was the first time just before the last time you remember saying it.

Cartoons

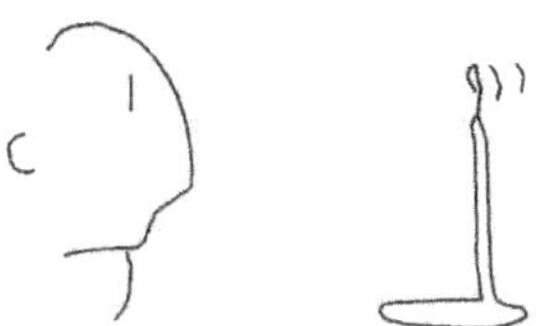

Snapshots of the Populous

TM
Robertson

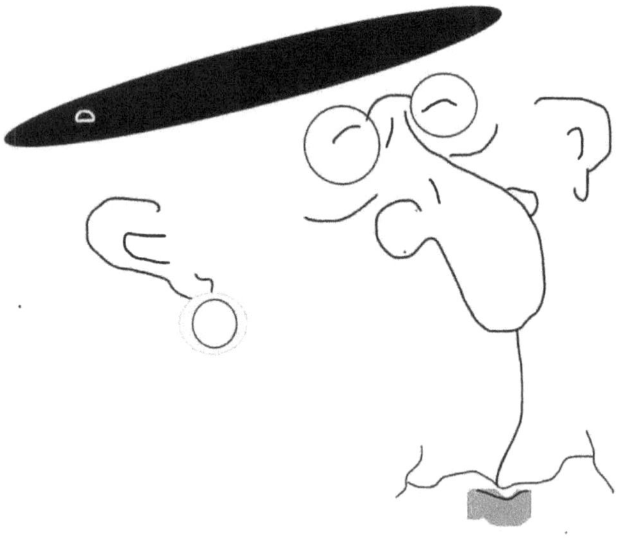

Although not the least bit talented,
Bernard figured the "Right Look"
was his ticket into art school

TM
Robertson

Snapshots of the Populous…

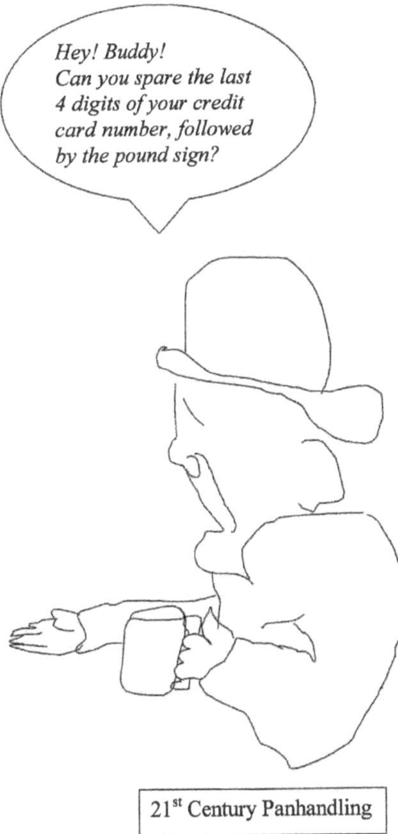

21st Century Panhandling

TM
Robertson

Snapshots of the Populous...

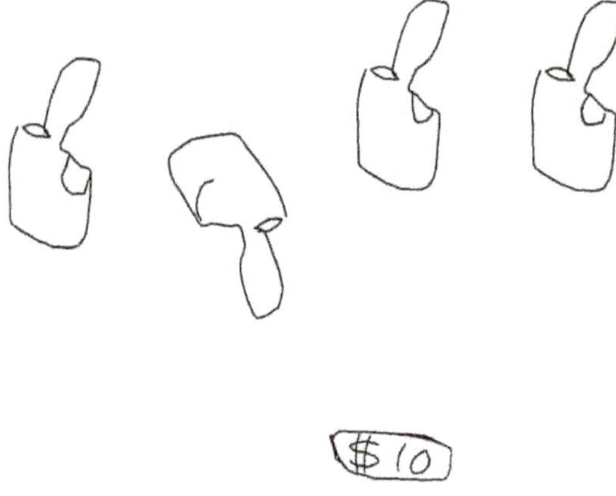

> Always the ultimate observationist,
> Irv exits the fireworks display ten bucks richer

Snapshots of the Populous…

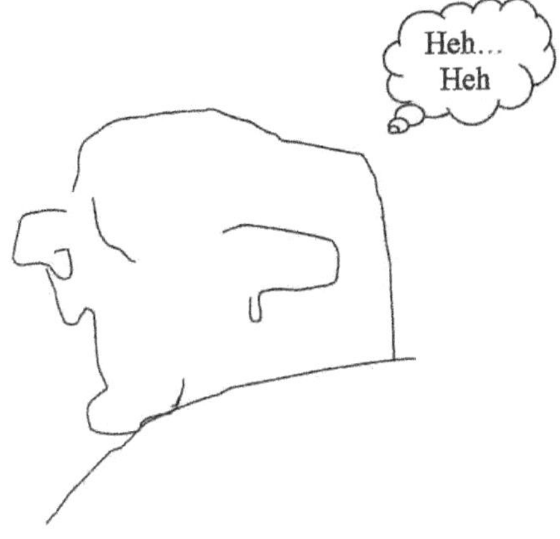

Although old, bald and toothless,
Winfield expended most of his energy
on recalling things that were funny at
the time…

TM
Robertson

Snapshots of the Populous…

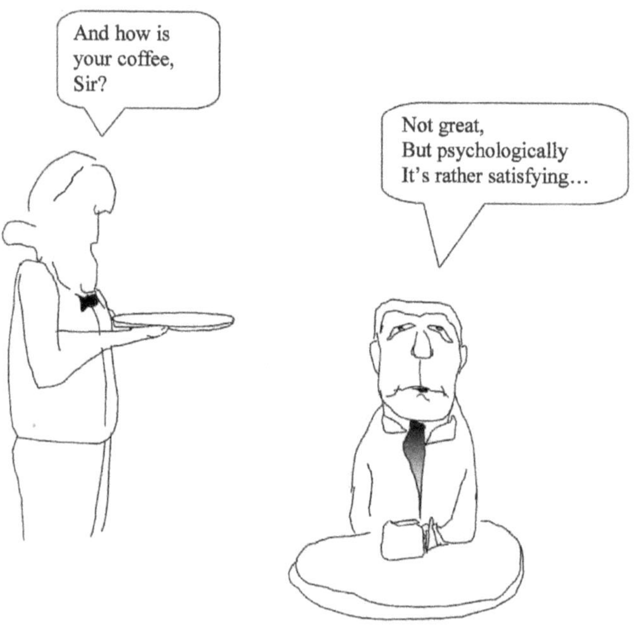

TM
Robertson

Snapshots of the Populous...

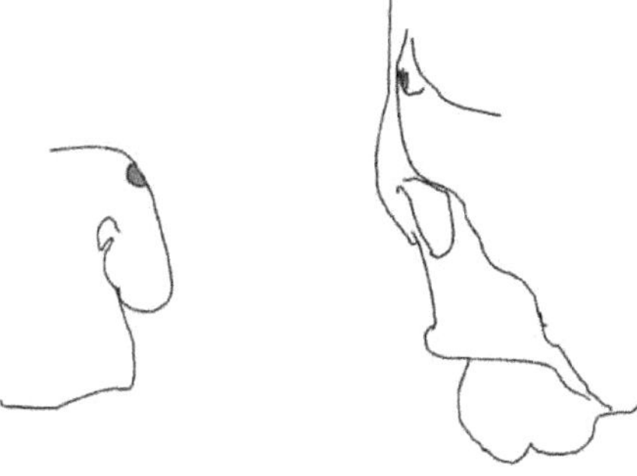

Older than time itself,
Jack and Manny engage in
perhaps the most primeval and
ritualistic form of warfare...
The Stare-down Contest

TM
Robertson

Snapshots of the Populous...

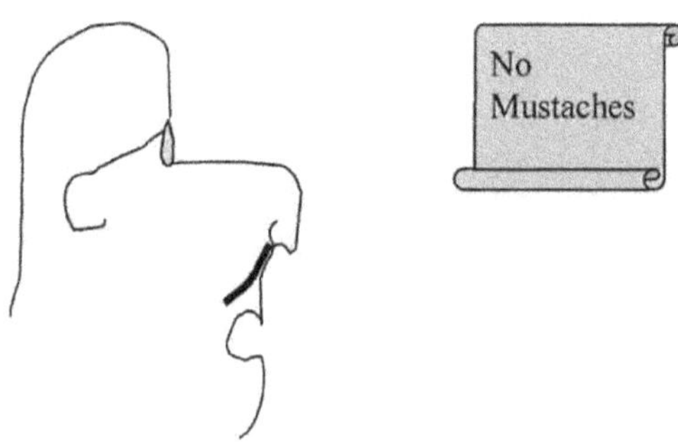

Challenged as he was when it came to hair growth,
Carl reacts to the recent change concerning the company mustache policy...

TM
Robertson

Snapshots of the Populous…

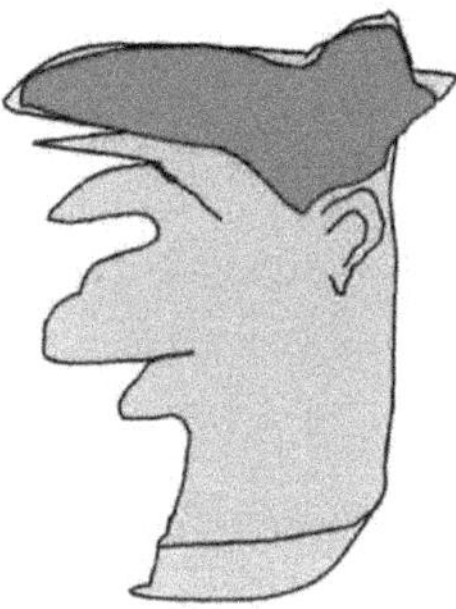

History is made as Cro-Magnon
man tries on the first-ever
toupee

TM
Robertson

Snapshots of the Populous...

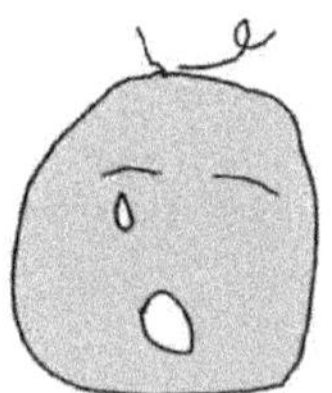

Baby-Jane absolutely
hated her new hair...

TM
Robertson

Snapshots of the Populous…

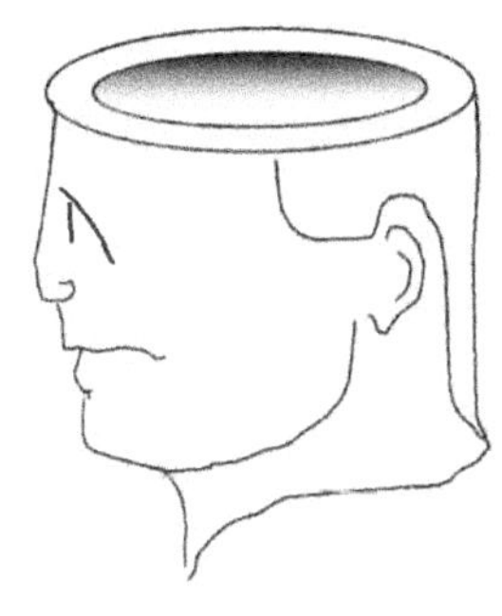

TM
Robertson

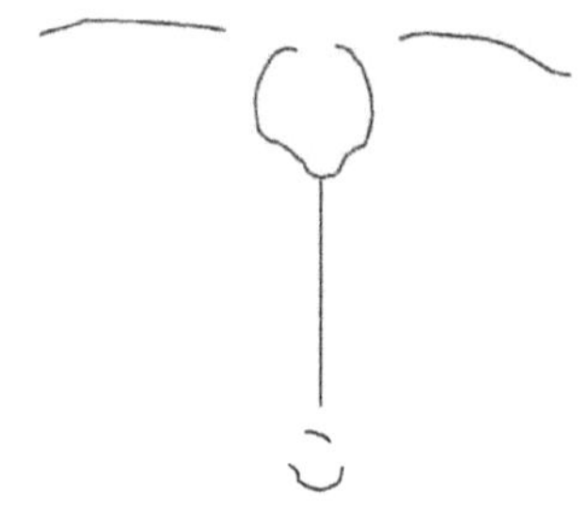

Kevin, reacting to the prospect
of actually eating spinach

TM
Robertson

Snapshots of the Populous…

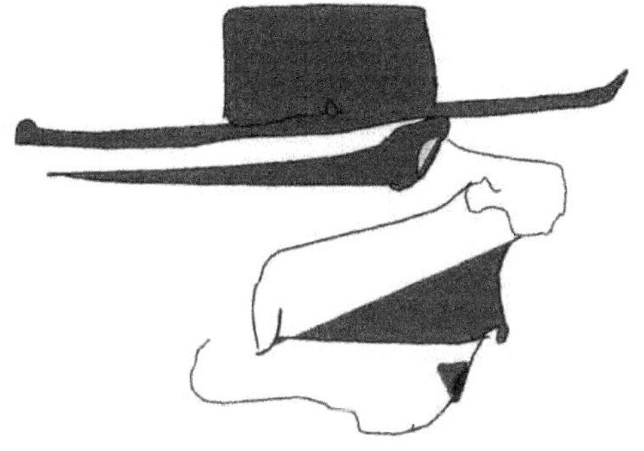

TM
Robertson

Snapshots of the Populous...

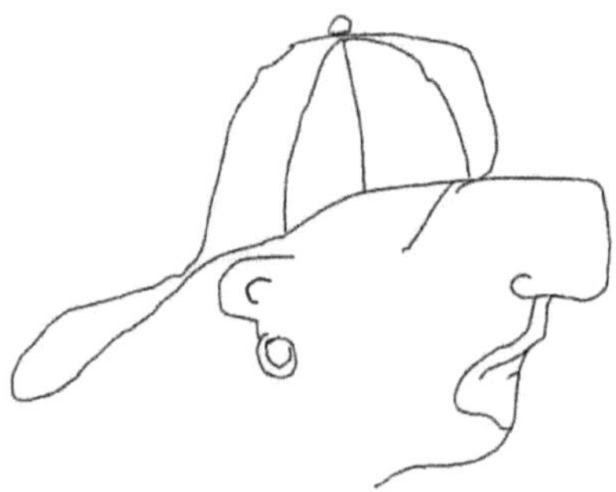

It was evident that Ed
would rather nurture a
trend as opposed to ever
actually setting one...

TM
Robertson

Snapshots of the Populous...

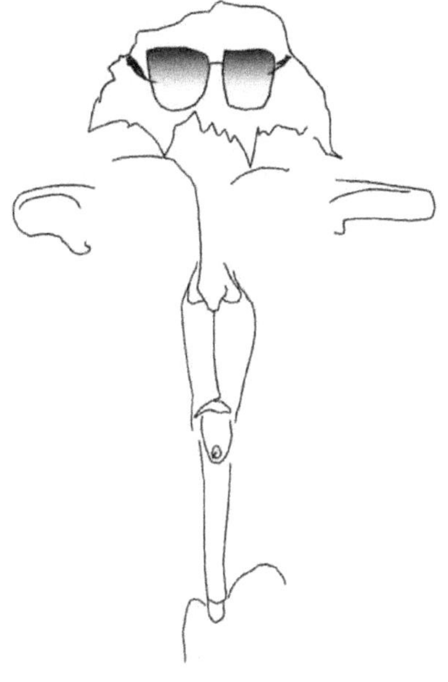

Benny, squirming under the
psychological weight of socially-
required, hair-planted sunglasses...

TM
Robertson

Snapshots of the Populous…

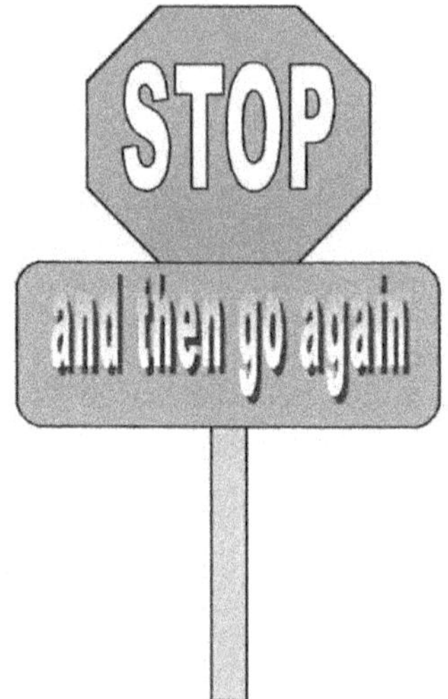

Street Signs for the obsessively literal

TM
Robertson

Snapshots of the Populous…

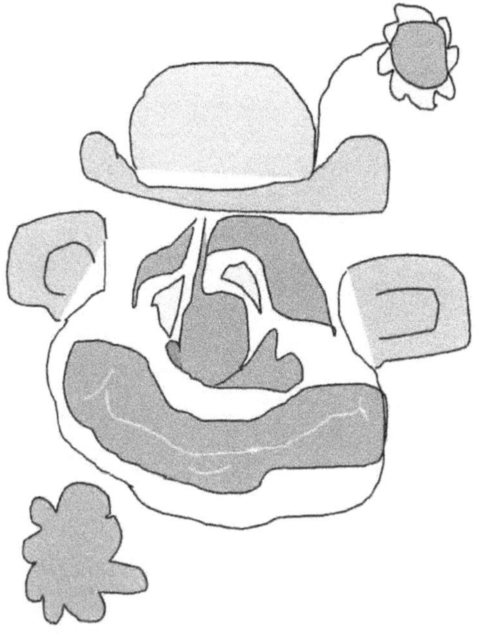

Although not employed as one,
he most certainly could have passed
for one

TM
Robertson

Snapshots of the Populous…

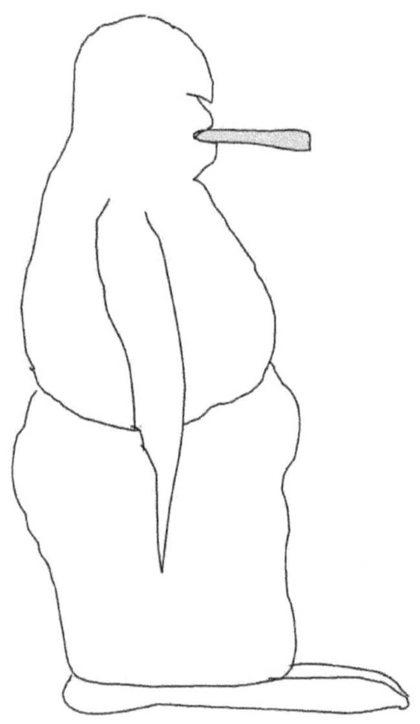

Al,
Displaying a single-minded
pleasure…

Snapshots of the Populous...

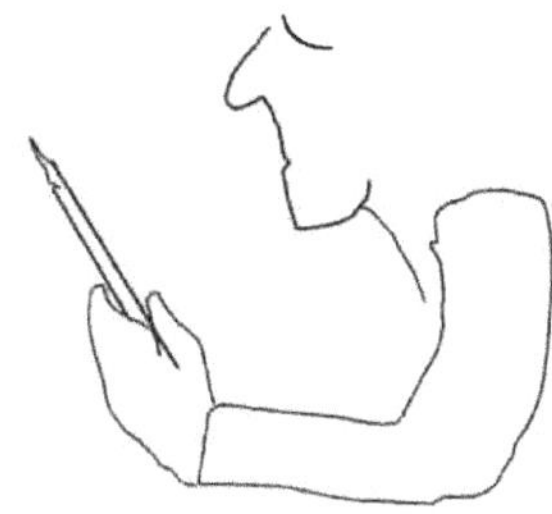

Carlton,
Finding nostalgia in a wooden pencil

TM
Robertson

Snapshots of the Populous...

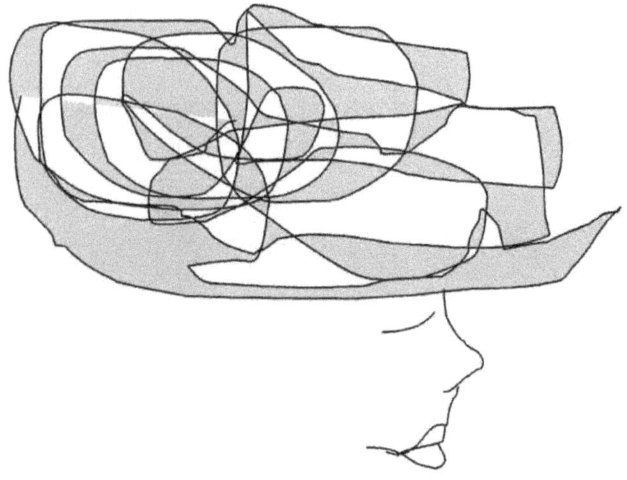

TM
Robertson

120

Snapshots of the Populous...

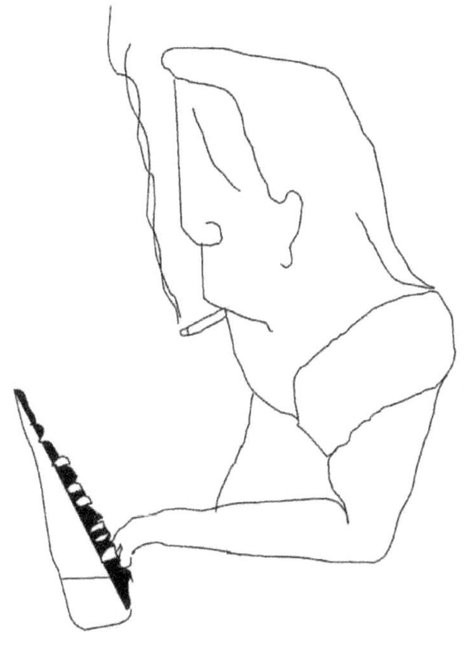

TM
Robertson

Snapshots of the Populous…

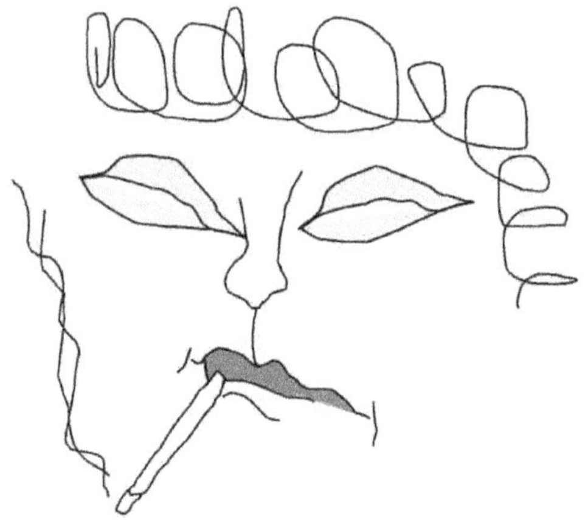

Generally speaking, Nadine was generally pissed…

TM
Robertson

Snapshots of the Populous...

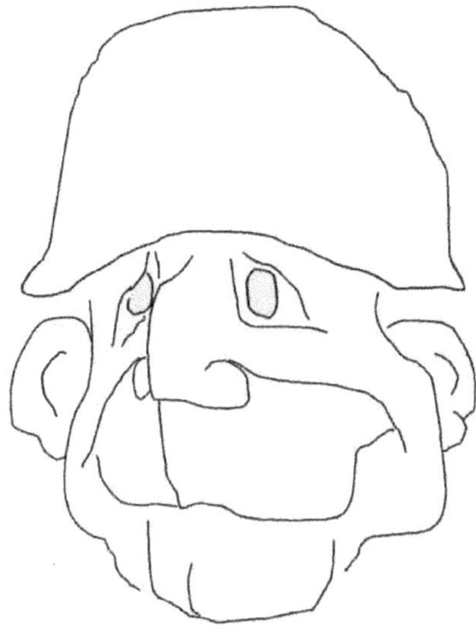

Although enamoured with his nifty, Army helmet collection, Billy actually found more pleasure in a nice new pair of colored contact lenses...

TM
Robertson

Snapshots of the Populous…

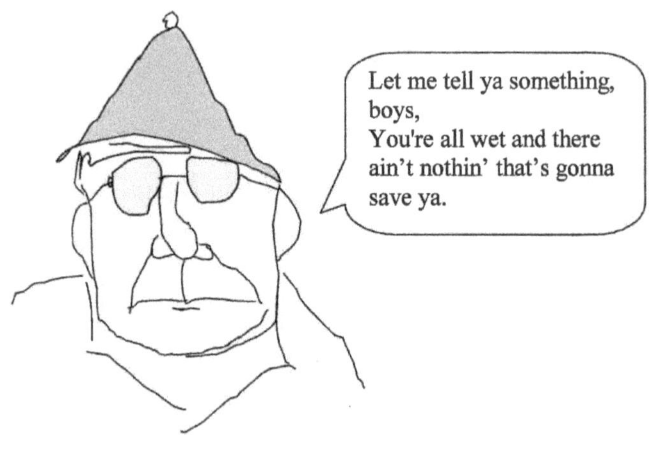

Forever the melodramatic, Rodney practices the soliloquy for the football team that he would never coach…

TM
Robertson

Snapshots of the Populous...

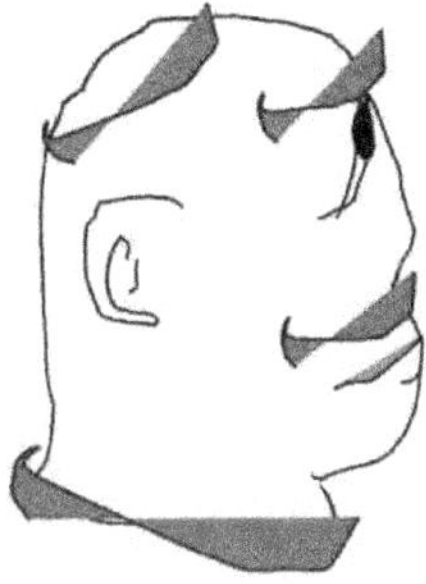

*It was clear that Leo's lone idiosyncrasy
had something to do with a certain shape...*

TM
Robertson

Snapshots of the Populous…

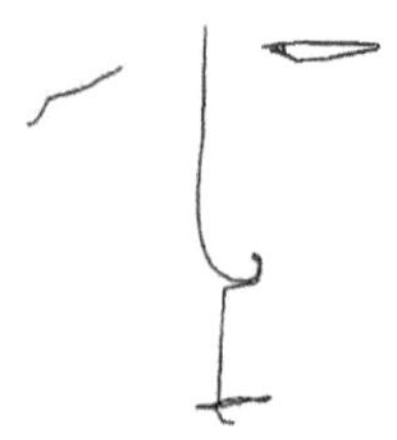

Jack, watching his right-eye nod-off

TM
Robertson

Snapshots of the Populous...

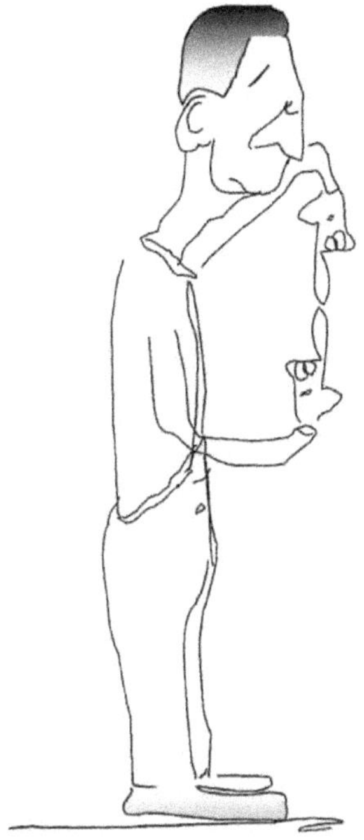

Kenny successfully establishes his own version of Yin Yang...

Snapshots of the Populous…

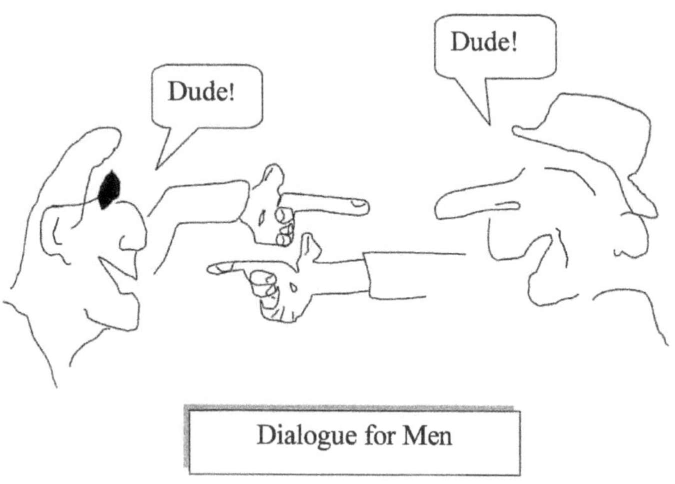

TM
Robertson

128

Snapshots of the Populous…

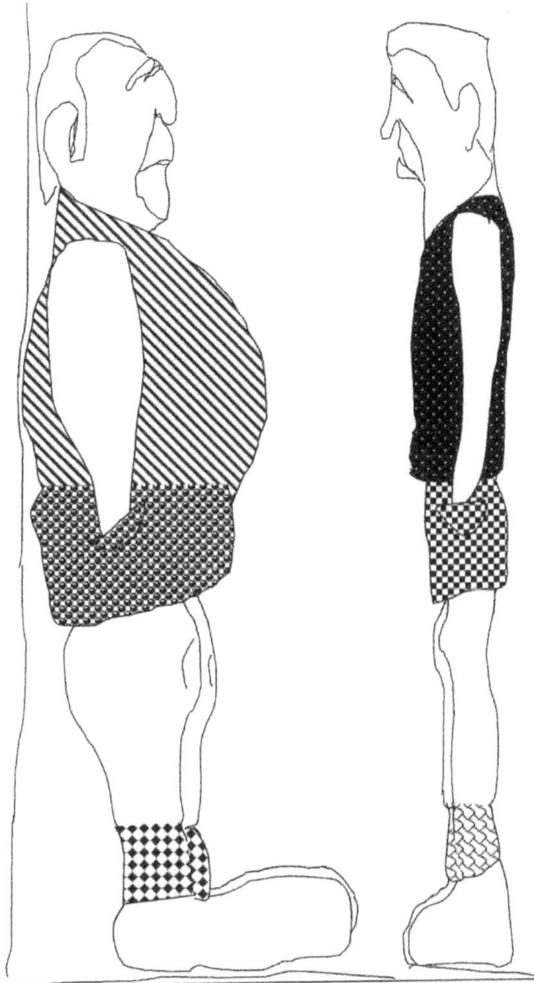

Having protested spousal involvement in their personal fashion selections, The Boys now ~ silently ~ cry out for help…

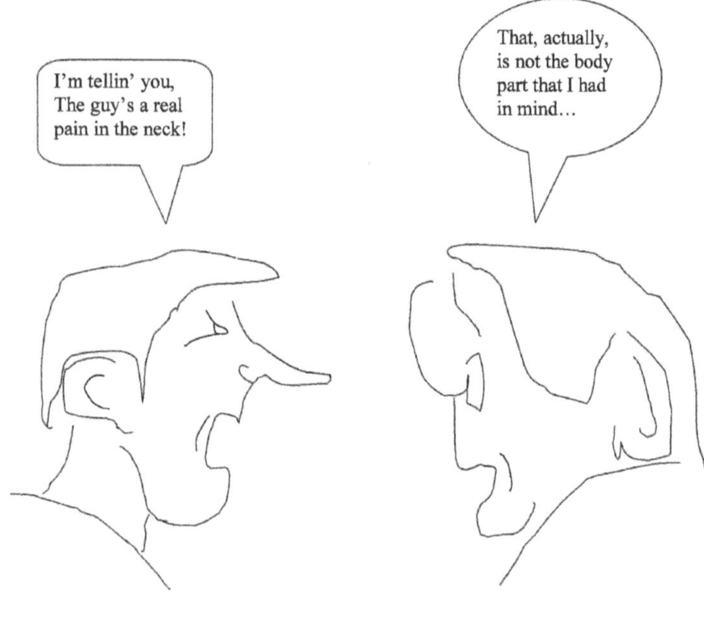

I'm tellin' you,
The guy's a real
pain in the neck!
That, actually,
is not the body
part that I had
in mind...
A classic case of utilizing the human anatomy to
select and denote certain personality types...
TM
Robertson

Snapshots of the Populous…

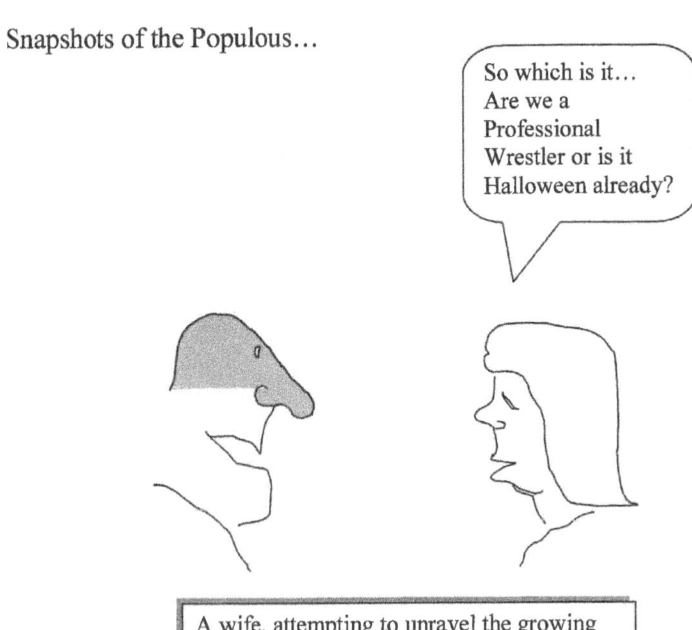

A wife, attempting to unravel the growing
complexities of her middle-aged husband…

TM
Robertson

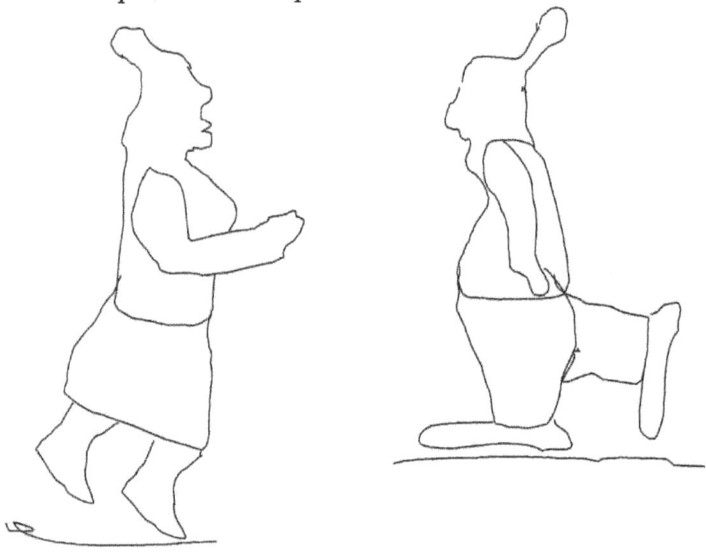

Sonja and Eddie found happiness in subtly influencing each other: For her it was his dance steps, and for him it was her hairdresser…

TM
Robertson

Snapshots of the Populous…

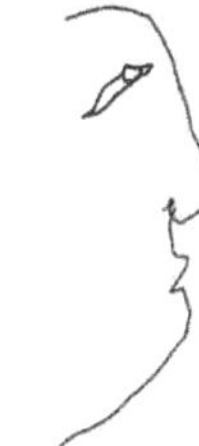

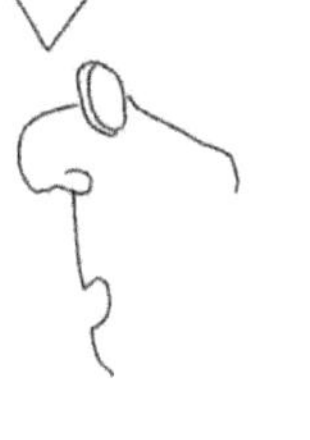

TM
Robertson

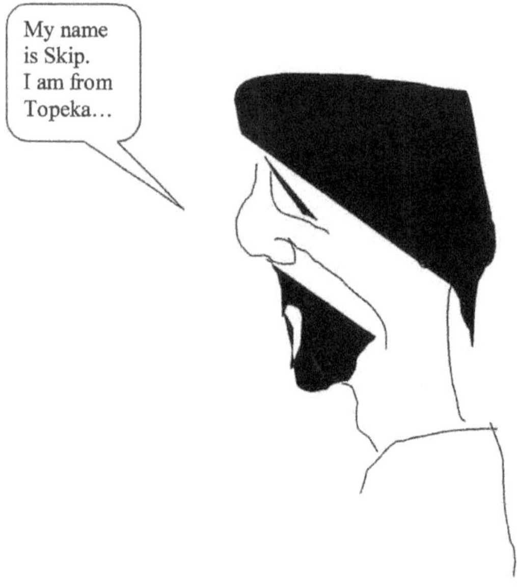

Confronted by the Coalition Forces,
An Iraqi guy remembers his lines.

TM
Robertson

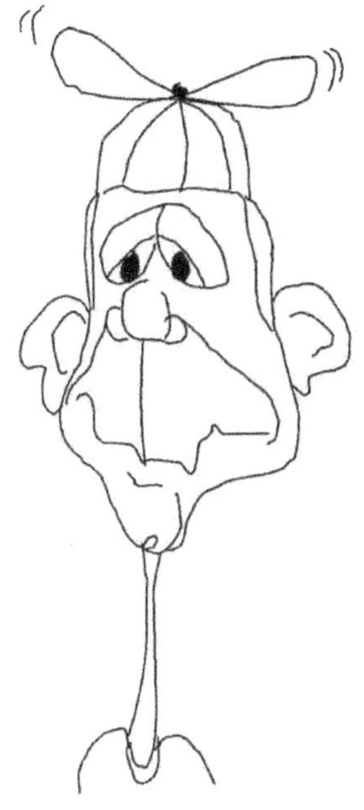

Sensing a slight whisper of wind,
Tommy toyed with the prospect of
actually being airborne…

TM
Robertson

Snapshots of the Populous...

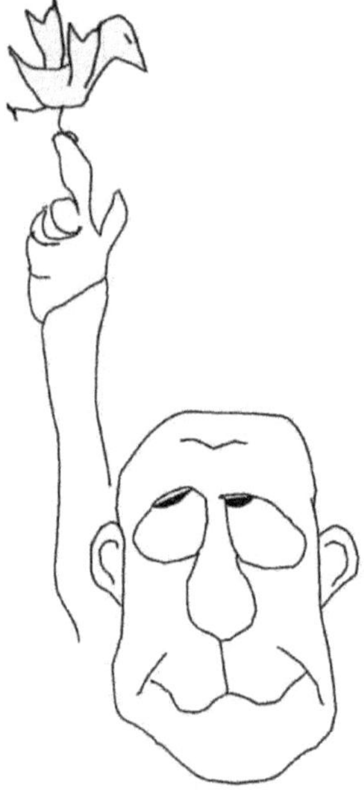

Snapshots of the Populous…

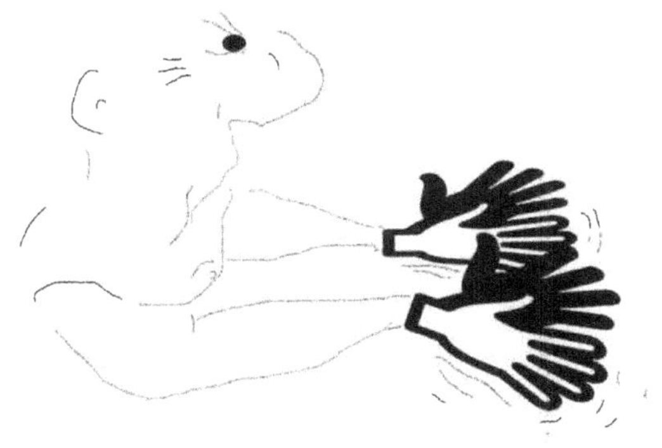

Very Intense Shadow Puppet
Practice

Snapshots of the Populous…

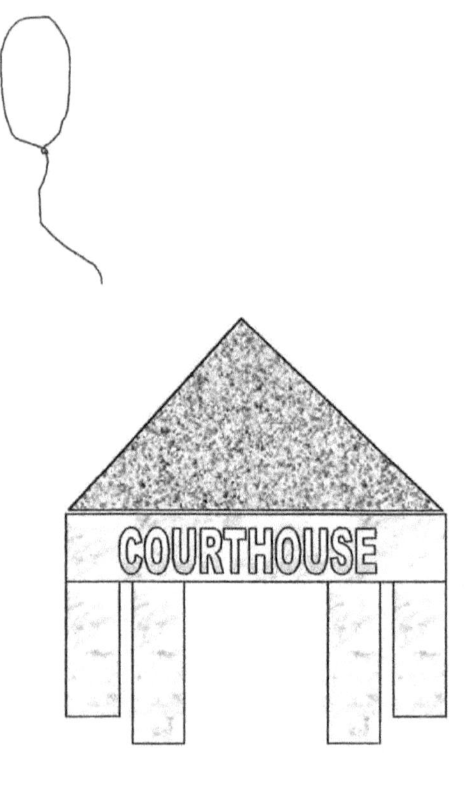

Trial Balloon

TM
Robertson

138

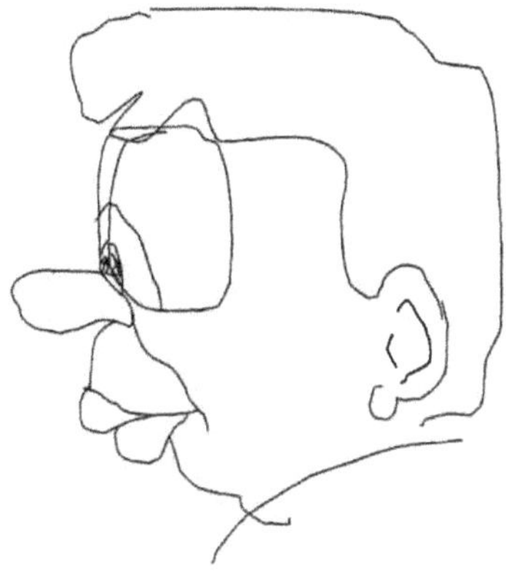

Unlike other former President look-a-likes, Phil fully enjoyed the notoriety, except for the occasional off-the-cuff foreign policy criticisms overheard while attending faux State Department functions

TM
Robertson

Snapshots of the Populous…

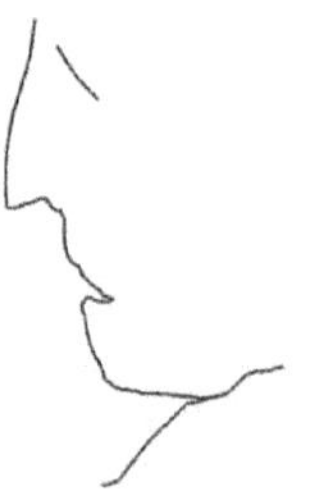

TM
Robertson

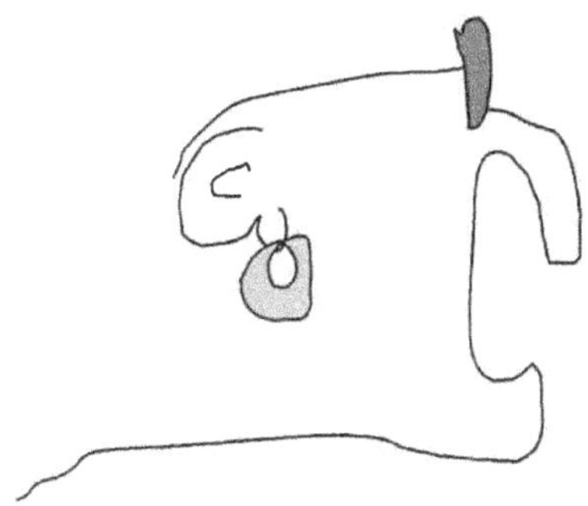

The strategic placement of Dunwoody's earring caused the rest of his face to inexplicably freeze up

TM
Robertson

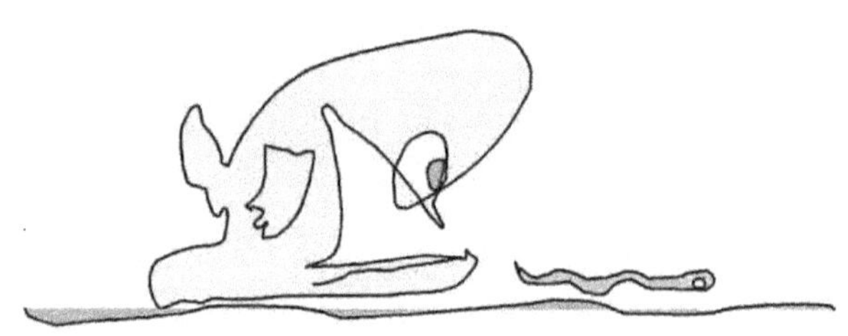

A classic case of the once temperate - yet now tempted - barnyard fowl about to fall off of the worm wagon

TM
Robertson

Snapshots of the Populous…

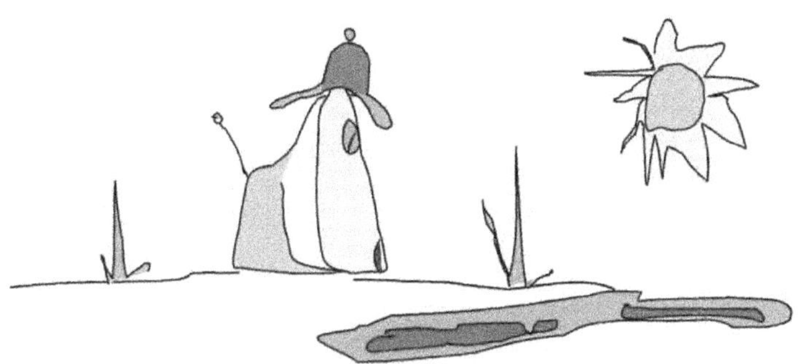

By day he was "Rex the Wonder Dog and Super-Sleuth".
Dispatched to exotic, far-off lands like this assignment investigating
surreptitious forms of plant life in the Sahara just outside of Cairo.
And by night he was just another unsuspecting neighborhood K-9…

TM
Robertson

Snapshots of the Populous...

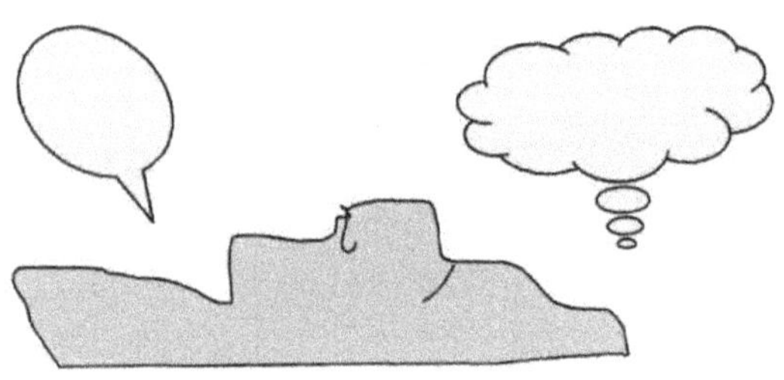

And as Melvin sleeps, he can neither think of anything nor think of anything to say...

Snapshots of the Populous...

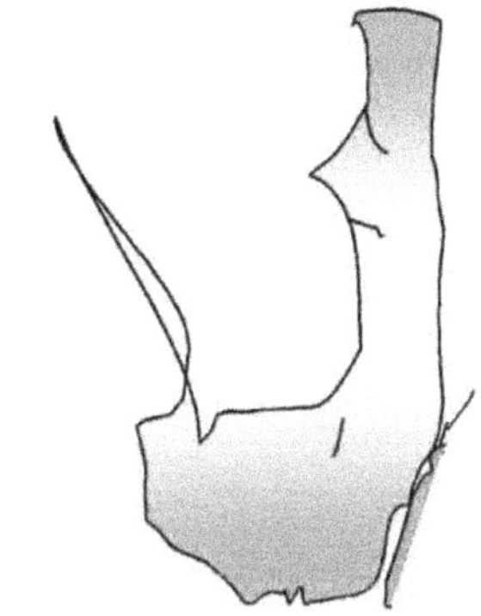

> **Terrance displaying a complete lack of interest in the propaganda of the day**

TM
Robertson

Snapshots of the Populous...

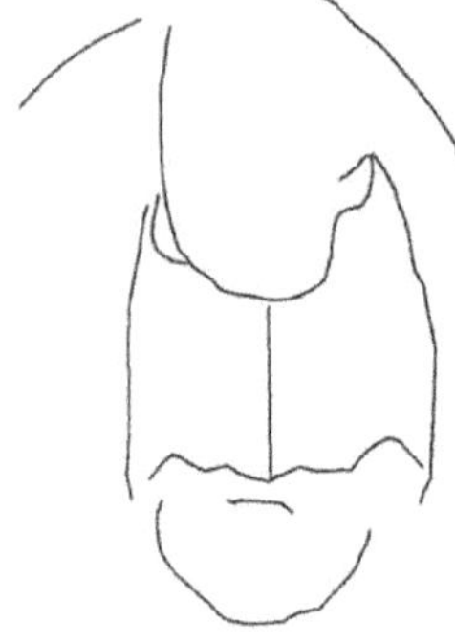

Uncle Bob,
Nodding-off after
merely glancing at the Sunday
paper...

Snapshots of the Populous...

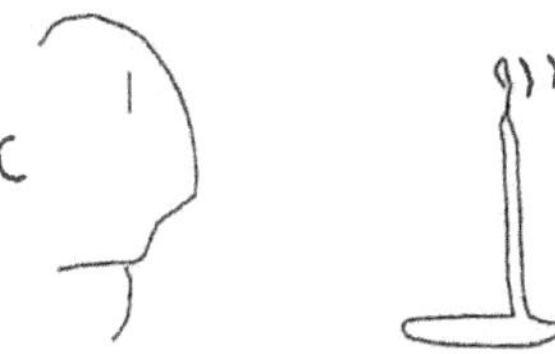

Ted:
Doing his level best to understand the subtle, scientific nuances and potential social significance of "candle power"

TM
Robertson

To be continued...
For the mind will remain forever curious